The Far Right in Greece and the Law

This book critically evaluates the rise of the far-right in Greece, detailing the legal context in which to understand both the emergence of Golden Dawn, the far-right's largest grouping, and the 2020 court decision in which it was deemed to be a criminal organisation.

Golden Dawn was a political party which, for years, also functioned as a violent subculture movement, with limited to no interference by the state. This book sets out the background to its rise in Greece, tracing its development from the post-Junta era. At the same time, the book provides an assessment of the legal framework within which the far-right has operated, and the legal tools available to tackle it – including criminal law, non-discrimination law, the laws governing political parties and the public order framework, and the country's international and European obligations. Golden Dawn functioned as both a political party and violent entity until its leadership and parliamentary members were found guilty of leading and participating in a criminal organisation. This book demonstrates that the state of impunity in which Golden Dawn's violent hit squads functioned was a facilitating factor for its rise, and potentially for its demise, as the group potentially felt untouchable. With its attention to the ways Greek Law has tackled, and failed to tackle, Golden Dawn, *The Far Right in Greece and the Law* offers a timely and more generally useful assessment of how legislation, courts and policies can best challenge the far-right.

This book will be of interest to those teaching and studying in law and politics, as well as others concerned with the rise of the far-right and violent organisations, especially in Europe.

Natalie Alkiviadou is Senior Research Fellow at Danish think-tank Justitia. Her research focuses on free speech, 'hate speech' and the far-right with two Routledge monographs and a range of peer-reviewed articles on the themes.

The Far Right in Greece and the Law

Natalie Alkiviadou

R Routledge
Taylor & Francis Group
a GlassHouse Book

First published 2022
by Routledge
4 Park Square, Milton Park, Abingdon, Oxon OX14 4RN

and by Routledge
605 Third Avenue, New York, NY 10158

A GlassHouse book

Routledge is an imprint of the Taylor & Francis Group, an informa business

British Library Cataloguing-in-Publication Data
A catalogue record for this book is available from the British Library

Library of Congress Cataloging-in-Publication Data
A catalog record has been requested for this book

ISBN: 978-1-032-26630-5 (hbk)
ISBN: 978-1-032-26661-9 (pbk)
ISBN: 978-1-003-28930-2 (ebk)

DOI: 10.4324/9781003289302

Typeset in Bembo
by Deanta Global Publishing Services, Chennai, India

Εις μνήμη του Σαχζάτ Λουκμάν και του Παύλου Φύσσα.
Προς τιμή όλων των γνωστών και άγνωστων θυμάτων
της Χρυσής Αυγής.
Ποτέ Ξανά

میں- یاد کی فیساس پاولوس اور لقمان ش‌ہزاد
میں- اعزاز کے متاثرین نامعلوم اور معلوم تمام ڈان کے گولڈن
ن‌ہیں کبھی دوبارہ.

In memory of Shehzad Luqman and Pavlos Fyssas.
In honour of all the known and unknown victims of Golden
Dawn.
Never Again.

فی ذکری شهزاد لقمان وبافلوس فیساس.
تکریما لجمیع ضحایا الفجر الذهبی المعروفین والمجهولین.
لکی لا یعید التاریخ نفسه.

For Markella and Andrew.
I love you forever.

Contents

Acknowledgements

This book is partly based on the PhD I defended in 2017 at the Vrije Universiteit Amsterdam. For this, I am forever grateful for the assistance given to me by Dr Uladzislau Belavusau and Prof. Gareth Davies. Following my defence and the ongoing trial of Golden Dawn, I continued working on the matter in preparation for the outcome of the trial and the day after.

Thank you to the reviewers of my proposal whose comments were very helpful in improving the book.

All errors are my own. All translations (and possible errors) from Greek to English are my own.

Chapter 1

Introduction

1.1 General Introduction

1.1.1 Aims and Structure

This book will map out the legal framework that can be utilised to challenge the far-right in Greece. The analysis will be effectuated against the backdrop of a contextual discussion, composed of three spheres. Namely, an overview of the country's legal and political system, as established by its constitution, which will facilitate an understanding of the subsequent analysis, looking at issues such as primary sources of law and the functioning and powers of the judiciary. Furthermore, given Greece's experience under a military dictatorship, and the ramifications this has had on the development of its legal framework and the far-right as a phenomenon, an insight into this period of history will be provided. An insight into the military dictatorship and the civil war will inform the discussion on the current treatment of political parties by the Greek legal system. The book will also set out the context of the far-right in Greece, looking at its development following the post-dictatorship period and its composition today. Once the contextual setting has been established, there will be an overview of the definitional framework of key terms, including racial discrimination and incitement to racial and religious violence, as these emanate from the country's legislation. There will then be an assessment of the treatment of political parties in the Greek legal order. Instead of integrating this in Chapter 3 on human rights (within the framework of the freedom of association), it will be a standalone chapter, given the centrality of the treatment of political parties in the Greek legal order to the substance of the book, the handling of Golden Dawn by the state and the impact an understanding of this treatment has on subsequent analyses and themes. The book will then look at the country's domestic legal framework in the realm of challenging the far-right. To this end, it will firstly pinpoint how the key freedoms of expression, assembly and non-discrimination

DOI: 10.4324/9781003289302-1

are established therein. The role of criminal law will then be appraised
in relation to the far-right, looking particularly at Law 927/1979 on
Punishing Acts or Activities aiming at Racial Discrimination, as revised
by Law 4285/2014 on Amending Law 927/1979 and the Transposition of
Framework Decision 2008/913/JHA on Combating Certain Forms and
Expressions of Racism and Xenophobia by means of Criminal Law. It
will assess the relevant provisions of the Greek Criminal Code, such as
those on racial aggravation and criminal and terrorist organisations. After
examining the relevant aspects of the national legal framework, the book
will consider the interpretation and incorporation of the country's obligations as these emanate from international and European documents. More
particularly, it will look at the status of the International Covenant on
Civil and Political Rights (ICCPR) and the International Convention
on the Elimination of all Forms of Racial Discrimination (ICERD) in
national law. In order to determine the state's adherence to international
obligations, potential reservations and/or declarations made on provisions
of international conventions will be assessed. On a Council of Europe
level, it must be noted that Protocol 12 (general prohibition of discrimination) to the European Convention on Human Rights (ECHR) was signed
by Greece in 2000 but has not yet been ratified. On a European Union
(EU) level, the analysis of the Framework Decision on Combating Certain
Forms and Expressions of Racism and Xenophobia by Means of Criminal
law[1] will not be discussed in the section on international and European
obligations but, rather, in the national legal framework as this tool has
amended the principal legal instrument that tackles issues relevant to challenging the far-right, namely Law 927/1979 mentioned above. This is also
the case for Law 3304/2005 on the Implementation of the Principle of
Equal Treatment regardless of Racial or Ethnic Origin, Religion or other
Beliefs, Disability, Age or Sexual Orientation, which transposed EU anti-
discrimination directives. Law 3304/2005 will be dealt with in the national
legal framework even though it transposes EU law given that it is the only
anti-discrimination legislation which exists in Greece. By considering all
of the above frameworks, this book incorporates all means and methods
directly or indirectly available to Greece for the purposes of challenging
the far-right. The book concludes on key themes, making reference to
the compatibility between national law and international and European

---

1 Council Framework Decision 2008/913/JHA of 28 November 2008 on Combating
   Certain Forms and Expressions of Racism and Xenophobia by Means of Criminal Law.

law and, more generally, appraising whether the current system is well-equipped to confront the far-right.

1.1.2 Contribution of the Book

Literature to date has looked at certain angles of the far-right in Greece, predominantly through the spectrum of political science. For example, Vasilopoulou and Halikiopoulou's 2015 *The Golden Dawn's Nationalist Solution – Explaining the Rise of the Far-Right in Greece*[2] contextualises the rise of Golden Dawn within the Eurozone crisis. The authors argue that the movement's success may be explained by the extent to which it was able to respond to the crisis of the nation-state and democracy in Greece with its 'nationalist solution.' In a 2020 book by Ellinas, *Organizing against Democracy: The Local Organizational Development of Far Right Parties in Greece and Europe*, the author explores how and why extreme parties succeed in some local settings while, in others, they fail. Several relevant books published in the Greek language include Psarras's *The Black Bible of Golden Dawn*,[3] which documents the history of this group and Hasapopoulos's *Golden Dawn – History, Personalities and the Truth*.[4] There have also been journal articles on Golden Dawn, such as Xenakis's 'A New Dawn? Change and Continuity in Political Violence in Greece' and Ellinas's 'The Rise of Golden Dawn: The New Face of the Far-Right in Greece.' The present book brings an added value since it looks at the far-right through a legal point of view by assessing the legal tools available on a national level in Greece to tackle the far-right as well as providing a critical overview of Golden Dawn, its rise and its demise. This is conducted against a contextual backdrop of the history and development of the far-right in Greece.

1.1.3 Contextual and Definitional Framework

1.1.3.1 Overview of Greek Political and Legal System

Greece is a parliamentary republic and adopts a civil law system. In 1924, following a referendum, the Monarchy was abolished and a new

---

2   Sofia Vasilopoulou & Daphne Halikiopoulou, 'The Golden Dawn's Nationalist Solution – Explaining the Rise of the Far-Right in Greece' (1st edn. Palgrave, London 2015).

3   Dimitris Psaras, 'The Black Bible of Golden Dawn: The Documented History of a Nazi Group' ('Η Μαύρη Βίβλος της Χρυσής Αυγής, Ντοκουμέντα από την Ιστορία και τη Δράση μιας Ναζιστικής Ομάδας') (1st edn. Polis, Athens 2012).

4   Nikos Hasapopoulos, 'Golden Dawn – History, Personalities and the Truth' (Χρυσή Αυγή - Η Ιστορία, τα Πρόσωπα και η Αλήθεια) (1st edn. Livani, Athens 2013).

constitution was adopted in 1927 which, amongst other things, established Greece as a parliamentary republic for the first time. However, in 1936, this form of government was abolished following the authoritarian rule of Ioannis Metaxas (4 August regime resulting from a self-coup).[5] The requirement of a new constitution following the socio-political turmoil created by the invasion and occupation of Greece by Nazi Germany in 1941 and the civil war that occurred from 1946 to 1949, led to the adoption of a new constitution in 1952, which established a constitutional monarchy. Following the fall of the military dictatorship which ruled between 1967 and 1974, the country went through a period of reform known as metapolitefsi (μεταπολίτευση). This period planted the seeds of public will and democracy, promoted political and individual rights as well as principles such as social solidarity, as reflected in the 1975 constitution in force today, amended in 1986, 2001, 2008 and 2019. The 1986 amendment focused on limiting presidential competences and, in 2001, the amendment was broad ranging, establishing new institutions and guarantees, which advanced the political and administrative system of the country and the ambit of human rights protection. The basic aim of the 2001 amendment was to bring the Greek constitution in line with European and international realities and obligations, which had emerged at the beginning of the century. The 2008 amendment included the repeal of the prohibition of any professional occupation of members of parliament (MPs) and allowed parliament to amend allocations to the state budget and monitor their implementation. The 2019 amendment incorporated nine changes, some of those dealing with the parliament, such as bringing the doctrine of parliamentary immunity in line with ECtHR case law on the matter.

The constitution provides that Greece is a parliamentary republic.[6] The legislative powers reside with the parliament and the president, the executive powers with the president and the government and the judicial powers with the courts.[7] The courts are not obliged to comply with legal provisions which they deem to be unconstitutional.[8] Article 30 provides that the president is the regulator of the state, elected by the parliament

---

5 Ioannis Metaxas is a controversial figure in Greek history because, on the one hand, he was a dictator but, on the other, he is admired for his famous rejection of Mussolini's Italy's request to allow the Italian army passage to occupy certain strategic places in Greece. This event continues to be commemorated with national parades in Greece and Cyprus.
6 Article 1(1) Greek constitution.
7 Article 26 Greek constitution.
8 Article 87(2) Greek constitution.

for a period of five years. The constitution is the primary source of law. Legislation may come from the parliament as well as from other authorities such as the president in the form of decrees and the ministers in the form of decisions, which are then approved by parliament.[9] Since 2019, legislative initiatives can be taken by the people, under certain conditions. The president promulgates and publishes the statutes and issues the decrees necessary for their execution. The president can issue general regulatory decrees which have the force of a statute.[10] The Supreme Administrative Court elaborates all decrees of a regulatory nature.[11] A body which is relevant and significant to the issues under consideration in this book is the Ombudsperson, an independent authority established under Article 103 of the constitution, with her/his role set out in Founding Law 2477/1997 on the Ombudsperson, Public Administration Inspectors and Auditors Body and subsequently enhanced by Law 3094/2003 on the Ombudsperson and other Provisions Law. In relation to the current study, the Ombudsperson has jurisdiction over public bodies for violations of principles of equal treatment[12] and conducts research and publishes special reports on the implementation and promotion of the principle of equal treatment without discrimination on grounds such as racial or ethnic origin or religious or other beliefs.[13] One such special report was a 2013 report on hate crime in Greece discussed later on in the book. The Ombudsperson cannot initiate or participate in judicial proceedings with its maximum powers being the referral of a case to the prosecutor or competent administrative authority for investigation.

Between 1974 and 2015, the Greek political scene was dominated by two parties namely the centre left PASOK – Pan-Hellenic Socialist Movement (ΠΑΣΟΚ – Πανελλήνιο Σοσιαλιστικό Κίνημα) and New Democracy (Νέα Δημοκρατία). Although since 2019, New Democracy is back in power, the rise of smaller parties has been facilitated due to the electorate's dissatisfaction in their social and financial policies, particularly their alignment with the

---

9   Article 73 Greek constitution, European Network of Legal Experts in the Non-Discrimination Field, Athanasios Theodoridis, 'Report on Measures to Combat Discrimination – Directives 2000/43/EC and 2000/78/EC – Country Report 2013 – State of affairs up to 1st January 2014' 6.
10 Article 43(2) Greek constitution.
11 Article 95(1)(d) Greek constitution.
12 Article 1 Law 3094/2003.
13 Article 5(3) Law 3094/2003.

Memoranda of Understanding(s).[14] A prominent example is that of SYRIZA – Coalition of the Radical Left (ΣΥΡΙΖΑ – Συνασπισμός Ριζοσπαστικής Αριστεράς), which was established in 2004 and is made up of left wing and radical left parties,[15] with those initially making up the party including a reformist party named Synaspismos/SYN – The Coalition of Left Movements and Ecology (Συνασπισμός/ΣΥΝ – Συνασπισμός της Αριστεράς των Κινημάτων και της Οικολογίας).[16] Synaspismos was founded in 1992 and defined itself as a 'pluralist left party of democratic socialism … placing a fresh emphasis on new issues, particularly feminism, democratic rights and the environment.'[17] Other organisations that made up this Coalition include AKOA – Renewing Communist Ecological (AKOA – Ανανεωτική Κουμουνιστική Οικολογική Αριστερά), DEA – The Internationalist Workers (ΔΕΑ – Διεθνηστική Αριστερά), KEDA – The Movement for the United in Action Left (ΚΕΔΑ – Κίνηση για την Ενότητα Δράσης της Αριστεράς) and Active Citizens (Ενεργοί Πολίτες). As well as these groups, SYRIZA attracted PASOK's[18] electorate following their disappointment with its role in the Troika's involvement in Greece and PASOK's links to corruption.[19] SYRIZA saw an impressive electoral rise from 2009 until 2015, going from 4.60% to 36.3% of the votes (first party).[20] Alexis Tsipras, leader of SYRIZA, was sworn in as prime minister in 2015, a seat which he retained until 2019. More on the fall of the two main parties (at least until 2019 in the case of New Democracy) and the space this gave to smaller parties will be discussed in the section on the electoral development of Golden Dawn.

14 A total of three Memoranda of Understanding have been signed between the European Commission (on behalf of the Stability Mechanism), Greece and the Bank of Greece. Financial support is given to Greece but under the condition that certain 'adjustments' are made (austerity measures).

15 Panos Petrou, 'The making of SYRIZA' (2012) Encyclopedia of Anti-Revisionism On-Line, <http://socialistworker.org/2012/06/11/the-making-of-syriza> [Accessed 1 November 2021].

16 Antonis Davanellos 'Where did Syriza come from?' (2012) http://socialistworker.org /2012/05/17/where-did-syriza-come-from [Accessed 2 May 2021].

17 Myrto Tsakatika & Costas Eleftheriou, 'The Radical Left's Turn towards Civil Society in Greece: One Strategy, Two Paths' (2013) South European Society and Politics, 9.

18 ΠΑΣΟΚ – Πανελλήνιο Σοσιαλιστικό Κόμμα - Panhellenic Socialist Movement.

19 http://blogs.lse.ac.uk/europpblog/2015/03/24/beyond-syriza-and-podemos-other -radical-left-parties-are-threatening-to-break-into-the-mainstream-of-european-politics/ [Accessed 6 May 2021].

20 2009: 4.60%, May 2013: 16.78%, June 2012: 26.89%, 2015: 36.34%: http://ekloges.news-nowgr.com/apotelesmata [Accessed 4 November 2021].

1.1.3.2 Dictatorship – Regime of the Colonels

On 21 April 1967, a group of far-right colonels carried out a *coup d'état*, which resulted in the country being run by a Regime of the Colonels (Καθεστώς των Συνταγματαρχών) also known as the Junta (Χούντα). It ended on 24 July 1974. The interrelation between post-Junta far-right groups with the Colonels' Regime had traditionally 'rendered them illegitimate in the eyes of Greek voters.'[21] In addition, the country's experience with the Nazi invasion in 1941 and its subsequent occupation rendered affiliation with fascist or Nazi ideologies unpopular. As such, the part of the electorate with far-right ideologies was attracted to the centre-right New Democracy as this option was considered more legitimate than resorting to supporting extreme-right parties.[22] Notwithstanding the above, by 2012 over 400,000 Greeks had voted for Golden Dawn, a party which embraced the principles enshrined in fascism and Nazism. The relationship between Golden Dawn and the Junta is clear since the links are present and obvious both historically and on a practical level. In 1973, Nikolaos Michaloliakos, the leader of Golden Dawn, joined the 4 August party (4η Αυγούστου) named after the date of Metaxas's self-coup in 1936. This party was founded by Constantinos Plevris, a far-right holocaust denier and LAOS (Λαϊκός Ορθόδοξος Συναγερμός – Popular Orthodox Rally) member of parliament (MP) who, in 2007, had been brought to trial for his book *Jews – the Whole Truth* (Εβραίοι – Όλη η Αλήθεια). Michaloliakos was arrested for political violence and convicted in 1978 for bombings in Athens. He remained imprisoned for ten months and during his stay met the leader of the Junta, George Papadopoulos. In 1984, Papadopoulos founded a new far-right party from prison, the National Political Union (Εθνική Πολιτική Ένωσις) and appointed Michaloliakos as leader of the party's youth wing.[23] In 1985, following a conflict between the two, Michaloliakos left this party. He then established the *Golden Dawn* magazine, which promoted ideas pertaining to National Socialism.[24] Moreover, on a practical level, leaders of the Colonels' Regime embraced Greek supremacist thinking, evident

---

21 Sofia Vasilopoulou & Daphne Halikiopoulou, 'The Golden Dawn's Nationalist Solution – Explaining the Rise of the Far-Right in Greece' (1st edn. Palgrave, London 2015) 21.

22 Ibid.

23 Human Rights First, 'We're not Nazis, but…The Rise of Hate Parties in Hungary and Greece and Why America should Care' (August 2014) 83.

24 Nikos Hasapopoulos, 'Golden Dawn – History, Personalities and the Truth' (Χρυσή Αυγή - Η Ιστορία, τα Πρόσωπα και η Αλήθεια) (1st edn. Livani 2013) 17.

in Golden Dawn's belief system.[25] Notwithstanding the above, and the established links between Golden Dawn members and the Junta, the former 'selectively mentions the Junta in its materials,'[26] aware of the general public's position when it comes to the country's experiences under the dictatorship. More on this era will be discussed when assessing its impact on the nature and content of Article 29 of the Greek constitution on political parties.

1.1.3.3 The Face of the Far-Right in Greece

This section will provide an overview of the phenomenon of the far-right in Greece following the fall of the Junta up until today. After 1974, far-right groups carried out violent activities such as bombings and personal attacks.[27] Even though many of the masterminds of the attacks were arrested, far-right violence of that period was 'largely under-recorded, under-reported and under-studied, in contrast with the violence of far-left groups.'[28] In relation to political participation, during this period, far-right parties had traditionally remained on the margins of the political system,[29] partly because of the reason stated above, namely the rawness of the public's wounds resulting from their experience with a far-right system, and the interconnection between the far-right and the Junta. The birth of the post-Junta far-right as a movement was essentially a 'reaction to leftist internationalism rather than … a positive identification with the Greek nation.'[30] Parties of this ideology which appeared on the scene include the Hellenic Front (Ελληνικό Μέτωπο), the Front Line (Πρώτη Γραμμή), National Democratic Union (Εθνική Δημοκρατική Ένωση), the National Alignment (Εθνική Παράταξη), the Progressive Party (Κόμμα Προοδευτικών) and the National Political Union (Εθνική

25 Human Rights First, 'We're not Nazis, but…The Rise of Hate Parties in Hungary and Greece and Why America should Care' (August 2014) 82.

26 Sofia Vasilopoulou & Daphne Halikiopoulou, 'The Golden Dawn's Nationalist Solution – Explaining the Rise of the Far-Right in Greece' (1st edn. Palgrave 2015) 58.

27 Robert McDonald, 'Pillar and Tinderbox: The Greek Press and the Dictatorship' (1st edn. Marion Boyars, New York 1983) 187–188.

28 Sappho Xenakis, 'A New Dawn? Change and Continuity in Political Violence in Greece' (2012) 24 Terrorism and Political Violence 3, 441.

29 Sofia Vasilopoulou & Daphne Halikiopoulou, 'The Golden Dawn's Nationalist Solution – Explaining the Rise of the Far-Right in Greece' (1st edn. Palgrave, London 2015) 20.

30 Antonis A. Ellinas, 'The Rise of Golden Dawn: The New Face of the Far-Right in Greece' (2013) 18 South European Society and Politics 4, 545.

Πολιτική Ένωση). The youth wing of the National Political Union became a 'breeding ground for future far-right leaders including Golden Dawn leader Nikos Michaloliakos.'[31] In general, the post-Junta far-right parties sought to 'protect the Helleno-Christian tradition but stayed short of the nationalist overtones that characterize the contemporary far-right in Greece.'[32] Examples of some form of political representation of the far-right include the 1977 national parliamentary elections, in which the National Alignment received 6.8% of the vote and five seats, the 1981 European parliament elections in which the Progressive Party received 1.96% of the vote and one seat,[33] and the 1984 European Elections when the National Political Union received 2.3% of the vote and one seat.[34]

In more recent times, the far-right scene was initially dominated by LAOS. LAOS was established in 2000 after its leader George Karatzaferis, a previous parliamentarian of New Democracy, came into conflict with the latter. Another founding member was the aforementioned Constantinos Plevris.[35] LAOS is 'explicitly nationalist and xenophobic,'[36] calling for the 'protection of the nation, the genus, the faith, the history and the cultural identity'[37] of Greece and for 'the expulsion of illegal immigrants.'[38] LAOS has also proved to be anti-Semitic with its leader publicly denying the Holocaust, uttering racist speech against Jews and relating Jews with the crime and theories regarding their world control through 'international Zionism.'[39] In 2002, the party included four Golden Dawn representatives on its local election listing.[40] In those elections, the party performed

31 Ibid. 546.
32 Ibid. 545.
33 Ibid. 546.
34 Ibid.
35 Kostas Pittas & Thanasis Kampagiannis, 'The Fascist Threat and the Fight to Eliminate it' (H Φασιστική Απειλή και η Πάλη για να την Τσακίσουμε' (2nd edn Marxist Bookshop, Athens 2013) 19.
36 Antonis A. Ellinas, 'The Rise of Golden Dawn: The New Face of the Far Right in Greece' (2013) 18 South European Politics and Society 4, 547.
37 Ibid. 137.
38 Ibid.
39 Anna Frangoudi, 'Nationalism and the Rise of the Far-Right' ('Ο Εθνικισμός και η Άνοδος της Ακροδεξιάς') (1st edn. Aleksandria, Athens 2013) 23.
40 Dimitris Psaras, 'The Black Bible of Golden Dawn: The Documented History of a Nazi Group' ('Η Μαύρη Βίβλος της Χρυσής Αυγής, Ντοκουμέντα από την Ιστορία και τη Δράση μιας Ναζιστικής Ομάδας) (1st edn. Polis, Athens 2012) 354.

well, receiving 13.6% of the vote in the Athens-Piraeus area.[41] LAOS entered the European parliament in 2004 with 4.12% of the vote and one seat,[42] the national parliament in 2007 with 3.8% of the vote and ten seats[43] and again in 2009 with 5.6% of the vote and 15 seats.[44] By 2012, the party's support decreased after it 'lost its outsider status'[45] following its support of the Memorandum of Understanding and its participation in the 2011–2012 government which worked on the second bailout. As a result, in May 2012, the party's vote dropped to 2.9% and 1.6% in June of the same year, resulting in it losing all its seats in parliament.[46] The participation of LAOS in Papadimou's government subsequently normalised the presence of Golden Dawn. Some of LAOS's electorate then supported Golden Dawn. This contributed to the fact that Golden Dawn was, to all intents and purposes, the only entity to inhabit the Greek far-right scene following the fall of LAOS. Given the domination of the scene by this party and the central role it plays in this book, it will be examined alone in the section below.

1.1.3.3 (I) GOLDEN DAWN – HISTORICAL DEVELOPMENT AND IDEOLOGICAL PROFILE

Before proceeding with describing the ideology of Golden Dawn it must be noted that following 2019 it has no electoral representation, and its street activity has fallen dramatically. The roots of Golden Dawn can be traced back to December 1980 when its leader, Nikolaos Michaloliakos, along with others he had worked with for the party 4 August and ENEK – Unified Nationalist Movement (ENEK – Ενιαίο Εθνικιστικό Κίνημα) issued the national socialist magazine *Golden Dawn*. The magazine

---

41   Election Results: <http://www.ypes.gr/el/Elections/CityElections/ResultsofElections/2002/> [Accessed 15 February 2021].

42   Election Results: <http://www.ypes.gr/el/Elections/ElectionsEuropeanParliament/ResultsofElections/2004/> [Accessed 15 October 2021].

43   Election Results (LAOS): < http://ekloges-prev.singularlogic.eu/v2007/pages/index.html> [Accessed 15 October 2021].

44   Election Results (LAOS): < http://ekloges-prev.singularlogic.eu/v2009/pages/index.html> [Accessed 15 February 2021].

45   Antonis A. Ellinas, 'The Rise of Golden Dawn: The New Face of the Far Right in Greece' (2013) 18 *South European Politics and Society* 4, 547.

46   Election Results (LAOS): < http://ekloges-prev.singularlogic.eu/v2012a/public/index.html#{"cls":"party","params":{"id":16}}> [Accessed 15 February 2021].

'espoused blatantly Nazi ideology'[47] and often glorified Hitler,[48] with its first issue in December 1980 stating that the group pursued a revolution for a Golden Dawn 'which will lead humanity again to nature and the Greek ideals of civilization.'[49] This was the beginning of a new life with 'no place for Zionists, their products and their agents.'[50] In a 1993 edition on racism, the magazine wrote that:

> Greeks are eminently racist ... Racism is not beating a negro in the street or burning a Filipina. Racism is the right to difference, the dislike of merger, the maintenance of a clean race and when we say clean race we mean the expulsion of foreign elements which do not conform with our nature and traditions.[51]

In 1983, the group running the publication of this magazine sought to organise itself into a political party and, so, Michaloliakos filed a declaration for the establishment of a political party entitled Popular Association – Golden Dawn (Λαϊκός Σύνδεσμος – Χρυσή Αυγή). Its statutes which were (voluntarily) deposited at the Supreme Court (more on this later) hold that it is a popular movement with 'faith in the ideology of nationalism.'[52] Golden Dawn promotes anti-Semitism and, as far back as the 1990s, was involved in violent activity, something which has been a characteristic of its actions as will be extrapolated below. Moreover, it endorses populist xenophobic and racist rhetoric with its statutes holding that it is 'against demographic alteration, through the millions of illegal immigrants and the dissolution of Greek society, which is systematically

---

47 Human Rights First, 'We're not Nazis, but…The Rise of Hate Parties in Hungary and Greece and Why America should Care' (August 2014) 82.
48 Council of Europe Commissioner for Human Rights – Report on Greece, CommDH(2013)6
49 *Golden Dawn* magazine, Issue 1 (December 1980): 'μια Χρυσή Αυγή που θα οδηγήσει και πάλι τον Άνθρωπο στην φύση και το Ελληνικό Ιδεώδες του πολιτισμού.'
50 Ibid.
51 *Golden Dawn* magazine (20/3/93) text entitled 'Greeks and Racism': Έλληνες και ρατσισμός – 'Ο Έλληνας είναι ο κατεξοχήν ρατσιστής…Ρατσισμός δεν είναι το ξυλοφόρτωμα ενός νέγρου στο δρόμο ούτε το κάψιμο ενός Φιλιππινέζου. Ρατσισμός είναι το δικαίωμα στη διαφορά, η αντιπάθεια της συγχώνευσης, η διατήρηση της φυλής καθαρής. Κι όταν λέμε καθαρή φυλή ενοούμε την αποτίναξη στοιχείων ξένων, αταίριαστων προς τη φύση και τις παραδόσεις μας.'
52 Statutes of the political party with the name 'Popular Association Golden Dawn' 'Καταστατικό του Πολιτικού Κόμματος με την Επωνυμία «Λαϊκός Σύνδεσμος Χρυσή Αυγή» pg.2.

pursued by the parties of the establishment of the so-called Left.'[53] It was founded and led by the same person who has been part of the Greek nationalist movement since the age of 16 and who was imprisoned in the 1970s for illegal possession of explosives. It embraces a biological conceptualisation of race and subsequently endorses biological as well as cultural racism underlining that 'for nationalism, the people is not just an arithmetic total of individuals but the qualitative composition of humans with the same biological and cultural heritage.'[54] In relation to how it was established, as noted by its leader in a 2012 interview

> we started in a Leninist way: we decided to issue a newspaper, Golden Dawn and build a party around it. Back in the 1980s we flirted with all sorts of ideas of the interwar years, including National Socialism and fascism. But by the 1990s we had settled the ideological issues and positioned ourselves in favour of popular nationalism.[55]

The party remained politically dormant up until 1993 when it capitalised on the issue of the name Macedonia to be given to a state of the Former Yugoslavia.[56]

In more recent years, the leadership attempted to avoid the reference to National Socialism in public speeches in an attempt to sanitise its image and attract a wider range of voters.[57] In the 2014 election campaign for example, Golden Dawn candidates disassociated themselves from violence, stopped uttering anti-Semitic speech and kept away from references to National Socialism, all with the hope of broadening the range of its electorate.[58] It can be said that, notwithstanding efforts to disassociate itself from National Socialism, this ideology not only continues to lie at the foundation of Golden Dawn but it is also the characteristic that sets it apart from the other post-Junta

53 Ibid.
54 Positions: political positions (Θέσεις: Πολιτικές Θέσεις) <http://www.xryshaygh.com /index.php/kinima> [Accessed 20 February 2021] Note the website is no longer functioning.
55 Antonis A. Ellinas, 'The Rise of Golden Dawn: The New Face of the Far-Right in Greece' (2013) 18 *South European Society and Politics* 4, 548.
56 Antonis A. Ellinas, '*The Media and the Far Right in Western Europe: Playing the Nationalist Card*' (1st edn. 2010 Cambridge University Press, New York).
57 Dimitris Psaras, '*The Black Bible of Golden Dawn: The Documented History of a Nazi Group*' ('Η Μαύρη Βίβλος της Χρυσής Αυγής, Ντοκουμέντα από την Ιστορία και τη Δράση μιας Ναζιστικής Ομάδας) (1st edn. Polis 2012) 250–251.
58 Ibid.14.

far-right entities[59] and from other far-right parties in the EU. However this move has been deemed 'superficial,'[60] with National Socialism remaining its ideological backdrop.[61] Even today, the party's symbol remains a Greek meander, which appears very similar to the Nazi swastika and its leader has often been seen using the Nazi salute.[62] As noted in the pre-trial report of the investigative judges drafted for purposes of requesting parliament to lift the immunity of Golden Dawn's MPs in the sphere of the party's trial (hereinafter pre-trial report), although the party alleged that its salute is an ancient Greek salute also used by (the dictator) Ioannis Metaxas, its National Socialist belief system is evident in, amongst others, its hidden constitution discussed below[63] and also in pictures depicting one of its MPs and seven other people with the Nazi swastika.[64] The National Socialist belief system of Golden Dawn was also referred to in the Prosecutor's recommendations to the Appeals Council (Συμβούλιο Εφετών) in the sphere of the trial (hereinafter Prosecutor's recommendations), through examples such as the Nazi salutes and evidence collected for the purposes of the trial including Nazi flags and Nazi military uniforms. Further, Golden Dawn adopts the Führerprinzip (leader principle) characteristic of the regime in Nazi Germany.[65] In fact, in the pre-trial report and Prosecutor's recommendations, reference was made to the absolute hierarchy and omnipotence of the leader.[66] Golden Dawn has demonstrated strong ties with the German neo-Nazi group, the Free South

59   Sofia Vasilopoulou & Daphne Halikiopoulou, 'The Golden Dawn's Nationalist Solution – Explaining the Rise of the Far-Right in Greece' (1st edn. Palgrave, London 2015) 16–17.

60   Vasiliki Georgiadou, 'The Electoral Rise of Golden Dawn. Revenge Vote of the Doubtful and the New Political Opportunities' ('Η Εκλογική Άνοδος της Χρυσής Αυγής. Ψήφος – Ρεβάνς των Επισφαλών και Νέες Πολιτικές Ευκαιρίες' in Giannis Voulgaris and Ilias Nikolakopoulos 'The Double Electoral Earthquake' (Διπλός Εκλογικός Σεισμός) (1 st edn. Themelio, Athens 2014) 185.

61   Ibid.

62   Fundamental Rights Agency, 'Racism, Discrimination, Intolerance and Extremism: Learning from Experiences in Greece and Hungary' (2013) 23.

63   Special Investigation Department: Athens Court of Appeal: Report to the President of the Greek Parliament regarding lifting the immunity of Golden Dawn Members of Parliament, Document Number 305 (19 February 2014) 20.

64   Ibid. 13.

65   Dimitris Psaras, 'Golden Dawn before Justice' ('Η Χρυσή Αυγή Μπροστά στη Δικαιοσύνη') (1st edn. Rosa Luxemburg Foundation, Berlin 2014) 37.

66   Special Investigation Department: Athens Court of Appeal: Report to the President of the Greek Parliament regarding lifting the immunity of Golden Dawn Members of Parliament, Document Number 305 (19 February 2014) 13–14, Prosecutor's Recommendation to the Appeals Council regarding the Prosecution of Golden Dawn members and Members of Parliament (15 October 2014) 32.

Network, inviting it to visit the Greek parliament.[67] As is the case with other neo-Nazi groups in Europe, Golden Dawn commemorates Adolf Hitler's birthday on 20 April each year.[68] It has also made statements glorifying the 'enlightened leadership of Adolf Hitler.'[69] Interesting deductions in relation to the nature of the party emanate from the secret statutes deposited at the Supreme Court for the purposes of the trial by journalist Dimitris Psaras.[70] It must be noted that Golden Dawn denied that this document belongs to it,[71] notwithstanding the fact that references had been made to it in the first editions of the *Golden Dawn* magazine issued over 20 years ago. However, it was relied upon in the pre-trial report and also in the Prosecutor's recommendations.[72] The statutes reveal that the party is founded on principles of National Socialism and biological racism that it inherently believes in the supremacy of the Greek race, endorses the leader principle and ensures a rigid hierarchy and strict discipline. For example, the statutes hold that the candidate members of Golden Dawn are 'only Aryans by blood, Greek by descent'[73] whilst a candidate may only be someone who 'accepts the ... principles of National Socialism and is determined to fight without reservation for their effectuation.'[74] They believe blood to be 'the supreme carrier of the biological virtue of our race.'[75] The statutes also underline the importance of the leader's principle holding that 'for us, the Greek national socialists there was never any dilemma, the democratic model of governance ... has no place in our movement ... we believe in the principle of the leader as

67   Fundamental Rights Agency, 'Racism, Discrimination, Intolerance and Extremism: Learning from Experiences in Greece and Hungary' (2013) 23.
68   Human Rights First, 'We're not Nazis, but...The Rise of Hate Parties in Hungary and Greece and Why America should Care' (August 2014) 83.
69   Dimitris Psaras, 'The Black Bible of Golden Dawn: The Documented History of a Nazi Group' (Ἡ Μαύρη Βίβλος της Χρυσής Αυγής, Ντοκουμέντα από την Ιστορία και τη Δράση μιας Ναζιστικής Ομάδας) (1st edn. Polis, Athens 2012) 40.
70   A journalist who has researched Golden Dawn extensively.
71   Special Investigation Department: Athens Court of Appeal: Report to the President of the Greek Parliament regarding lifting the immunity of Golden Dawn Members of Parliament, Document Number 305 (19 February 2014) 13–14.
72   Ibid. 26.
73   Άρθρο 12. 1: 'υποψήφια μέλη της χρυσής αυγής δύνανται να είναι μόνο Άριοι κατά το αίμα, έλληνες στην καταγωγή.'
74   Άρθρο 1.2: 'Στην Χρυσή Αυγή εντάσσεται ως δόκιμο μέλος οποίος αποδέχεται τις κοσμοθεωρητικές βιοθεωρητικές και πολιτικές αρχές του εθνικοσοσιαλισμού και είναι αποφασισμένος να αγνωιστή χωρίς συμβιβασμούς για την πραγμάτωσή τους.'
75   Άρθρο 4: 'Το αίμα είναι ο υπέρτατος φορέας των βιολογικων αρετών της φυλής μας.'

fundamental for state legitimacy.[76] They also provide that 'discipline which emanates from the hierarchy of Golden Down is necessary for the effectuation of the objectives of the movement.'[77] Interestingly, the Prosecutor's recommendations highlighted that the belief system of the party's members, including the MPs was 'criminally indifferent.'[78] They also refer to the militant and hierarchal structure of this group.[79] Furthermore, the pre-trial report referred to evidence of paramilitary elements to this group which depicts members of Golden Dawn carrying out military training including gun use, targeting, combat, self-defence and provision of first aid. Further, the self-sacrifice of members for the purposes of ensuring the objectives of the party are noted in Article 10 of its secret constitution. As noted, this party is 'no ordinary ultra nationalist party. No other extreme-right party in Europe is as stridently racist, nativist and violent, none is so unapologetically anti-Semitic, and none so openly calls for the overthrow of the state.'[80]

In addition to the National Socialist foundation of Golden Dawn, it is 'against parliamentary democracy and treats it with contempt,'[81] with Michaloliakos stating directly that 'we reject democracy.'[82] The party

76 *Attorneys of the Civil Action: Memo of the Civil Action of the Anti-Fascist Movement for the Trial of Golden Dawn (Υπόμνημα της Πολιτικής Αγωγής του Αντιφασιστικού Κινήματος για τη Δίκη της Χρυσής Αυγής)* (1st edn. Marxist Bookshop, Athens 2015) 20.
    'Για μας τους έλληνες εθνικοσοσοαλιστές δεν υπήρξε ποτέ κανένα δίλλημα, ο δημοκρατικός τρόπος διακυβερνήσεως, ο βασιζόμενος στην τυχάρπαστη πλειοψηφία των πολλών δεν είχε θέση στο κίνημά μας.... πιστεύουμε στην αρχή του αρχηγού ως θεμέλιο πολιτειακής νομιμότητας.'
77 Άρθρο 10: 'Η πειθαρχία που διέπει την ιεραρχική δομή της Χρυσής Αυγής είναι αδήριτη ανάγκη για την πραγματοποίηση των σκοπών της κινήσεως και αποτελεί συνειδητοποιημένη κατάσταση για κάθε μέλος.'
78 Prosecutor's Recommendation to the Appeals Council regarding the Prosecution of Golden Dawn members and Members of Parliament (15 October 2014) 26.
79 Special Investigation Department: Athens Court of Appeal: Report to the President of the Greek Parliament regarding lifting the immunity of Golden Dawn Members of Parliament, Document Number 305 (19 February 2014) 13–14, Prosecutor's Recommendation to the Appeals Council regarding the Prosecution of Golden Dawn members and Members of Parliament (15 October 2014) 30.
80 30 October 2013: Press conference of the Director of Internal Affairs (of the Police) Panagiotis Stathis following the investigation of accusations of police and Golden Dawn cooperation. Cited in Human Rights First, 'We're not Nazis, but…The Rise of Hate Parties in Hungary and Greece and Why America should Care' (August 2014) 87.
81 Council of Europe Commissioner for Human Rights – Report on Greece, CommDH (2013) 6, 4-3.
82 Nikolaos Michaloliakos, 'For a Great Greece in a Free Europe' ('Για μια Μεγάλη Ελλάδα σε μια Ελεύθερη Ευρώπη) (2nd edn. Ascalon 2000) 17 'Αρνούμαστε τη δημοκρατία.'

has not tried to hide this characteristic, with an example being the party spokesman's statement in 2012 in which he said

we do not like the petty MP posts, we do not want them at all. Of course we take advantage of some privileges of this membership, we now have a permit for a firearm, there is no possibility for an immediate arrest upon the commission of a criminal offence and it is a bit easier for us to move around.[83]

Further, in one of its magazine's issues, it held that, 'we say yes to everyone, we become the good guys of the system, we bless, with every way … the guilty political system … but we have a goal to use our actions as the Trojan Horse and destroy the system.'[84] As such, the MPs of this party 'consciously try to devaluate the parliament, the institutions and principles of the state.'[85]

Further, Golden Dawn is 'staunchly and indiscriminately anti-immigrant.'[86] Its statutes, as deposited by the party to the Supreme Court, hold that the party is 'against the demographic alteration, through the millions of illegal immigrants and the dissolution of Greek society, which is systematically pursued by the parties of the establishment of the so-called left.'[87] Parliamentarians of this party were quick and consistent in demonstrating their racist belief system with ample examples existing to illustrate this point. In 2012, a Golden Dawn MP Eleni Zaroulia referred to migrants in Greece as 'sub-humans who have invaded our country, with all kinds of diseases.'[88] It is noteworthy that no measures were taken against her by the Greek parliament. This is unlike the European

---

83 Statement made on 25/11/2012 in Crete: «Δεν γουστάρουμε τα βουλευτιλίκια… Εκμεταλλευόμαστε τα προνόμια αυτής της ιδιότητας. Έχουμε οπλοφορία πλέον με άδεια. Δεν έχει αυτόφωρο αν γίνει κανένα επεισόδιο και είμαστε πιο άνετοι στις κινήσεις μας».

84 Golden Dawn Magazine issue 134/2007: 'Λέμε ναι σε όλους, γινόμαστε καλάπαιδιά του συστήματος, ευλογούμε με κάθε τρόπο και με όλα τα "Κύριεελέησον" που διαθέτουμε το ένοχο πολιτικό σύστημα και όλα αυτά ασφαλώς με τοαζημίωτο, αλλά έχουμε σκοπό να χρησιμοποιήσουμε τις ενέργειές μας σαν Δούρειοίππο για να αλώσουμε το σύστημα…'

85 Prosecutor's Recommendation to the Appeals Council regarding the Prosecution of Golden Dawn members and Members of Parliament (15 October 2014), 110.

86 Sofia Vasilopoulou & Daphne Halikiopoulou, 'The Golden Dawn's Nationalist Solution – Explaining the Rise of the Far-Right in Greece' (1st edn. Palgrave, London 2015) 3.

87 Antonis A. Ellinas, 'The Rise of Golden Dawn: The New Face of the Far Right in Greece' (2013) 18 South European Politics and Society 4, 545.

88 Statement made in parliament in 2012: «Κάθε λογής υπάνθρωπο που έχει εισβάλει στην πατρίδα μας και με τις κάθε λογής αρρώστιες που κουβαλάει».

parliament where, in 2016, Martin Schulz expelled Golden Dawn MP Eleftherios Synadinos following his remarks that Turks are 'barbarians,' 'dirty' and 'dogs.'[89] The hateful stance of Golden Dawn has not been restricted to words only but is evident in its exclusionary activities and violence. More particularly, over the last few years Golden Dawn has provided welfare services such as health services, soup kitchens, blood donation and job centres for Greeks only.[90] By doing so, Golden Dawn has sought to appear to be supporting the (Greek) people, making up for the deficient social infrastructure during the financial crisis. The party also alleged to have funded these activities through the salaries of the MPs thus 'alluding to the ultimate ideals of sacrifice, selflessness and popular supremacy.'[91] Golden Dawn has 'accused' Jews or Zionists of attempting to eradicate Greece through globalisation.[92] Examples of such a belief can be reflected in the recital of a passage from the Elders of Zion by (now imprisoned) MP Elias Kasidiaris. It is anti-Roma, with examples of its actions including the support of a demonstration against the registration of 30 Roma pupils in a school in Lamia in 2012.[93] It has also disseminated hate against the Muslim minority of Turkish origin who live in Thrace with members of this community having reported hate speech, threats and violence carried out by Golden Dawn.[94] It is homophobic and transphobic.[95] In its 2015 report on Greece, the European Commission against Racism and Intolerance (ECRI) underlined that there was an increase in hate speech which was directly linked to the

89 9 March 2016: The president of the European Parliament, Martin Schulz, expelled the MP, explaining that his decision was in accordance with the article 165 of the EU. "It is a blatant violation of human rights upon which the EU is unswerving and bows to. (Here), there is an effort to outflank the red lines, so that racism becomes acceptable. But this is not happening from me." Schulz said: "So, according to article 165 of the regulation, in combination with article 11, Mr. Synadinos is excluded immediately from the session and the chamber."

90 Sofia Vasilopoulou & Daphne Halikiopoulou, 'The Golden Dawn's Nationalist Solution – Explaining the Rise of the Far-Right in Greece' (1st edn. Palgrave, London 2015) 58.

91 Ibid.

92 See for example: Apostolos Karaiskos 'Zionism and Globalisation' ('Σιωνισμός και Παγκοσμιοποίηση') (2012): <http://www.xryshaygh.com/enimerosi/view/siwnismos-kai -pagkosmiopoihsh> [Accessed 30 January 2021].

93 Council of Europe Commissioner for Human Rights – Report on Greece, CommDH (2013)6, 3.

94 Ibid. 11.

95 As reflected in, for example, the discriminatory talks that accompanied parliamentary debate regarding the passing of the civil union in Greece.

rise of Golden Dawn.[96] In light of the above, Golden Dawn has been described as belonging to the 'extreme right category of the broader far-right label'[97] due to the embracement of Nazi ideals, its dangerous approach to democracy and its anti-immigrant, anti-minority rhetoric.

1.1.3.3 (II) GOLDEN DAWN AND VIOLENCE

Although its violence fell substantially after the arrest of its leadership and some of its members, Golden Dawn has systematically used violence to instil fear amongst its political opponents and those groups it considers to be sub-humans (using the words of its MP Zaroulia as referred to above). Targets of Golden Dawn were initially political opponents such as leftists but, in the years that followed, other groups such as refugees and migrants were incorporated therein,[98] with multiple attacks being recorded over the following years, with such violence remaining unpunished for a long period of time.[99] Further, ethnic minorities such as Roma have been targeted, with incidences of violence being recorded against Muslim minorities in Thrace and persons belonging to the LGBTQ+ community. Golden Dawn's violence was carried out by its hit squads (τάγματα εφόδου), composed of members with particular physical features, knowledge of martial arts and use of weapons, especially trained in hard conditions. The members would wear black clothes or clothes with military colours, with the logo of Golden Dawn, military boots and helmets with short or no hair, possessing weapons such as knives, iron bars and bats.[100] A particularly significant description of the violence carried out by Golden Dawn was put forth by the president of the National Commission on Human Rights[101] for the purposes of the pre-trial report. He held that the violence conducted by Golden Dawn, which

---

96 European Commission against Racism and Intolerance: Report on Greece (24 February 2015) para. 34.

97 Sofia Vasilopoulou & Daphne Halikiopoulou, 'The Golden Dawn's Nationalist Solution – Explaining the Rise of the Far-Right in Greece' (1st edn. Palgrave, London 2015) 6.

98 Katerina Toidou & Giorgos Pittas, 'Golden Dawn's File – Neo Nazi Crimes and How to Stop them' ('Φάκελος Χρυσή Αυγή – τα Εγκλήματα των Νεοναζί και πως να τους Σταματήσουμε') (1st edn. Marxist Bookshop, Athens 2013) 15.

99 Ibid.13.

100 Prosecutor's Recommendation to the Appeals Council regarding the Prosecution of Golden Dawn members and Members of Parliament (15 October 2014) 42.

101 The National Commission on Human Rights is an independent advisory body to the state specialised in human rights issues.

is a centrifugal element of the party's public appearance, works on two levels. Firstly, there is the public violence in which members of Golden Dawn carry out violent acts, such as those carried out against market stalls of immigrants, often recording and uploading them on the internet as a form of the party's identity and success. There is also the secret type of violence which occurs at night and is directed at more vulnerable groups such as refugees.[102] Unlike its electoral development which was slow and fractured, Golden Dawn's use of violence became apparent more quickly, commencing in 1987 and becoming more systematic by 1992.[103] Essentially, up until the early 2000s, this party worked as a violent sub-culture working on the streets, remaining electorally marginalised. The backdrop which facilitated this was the fact that 1992 was the year during which a 'nationalist and xenophobic wave erupted'[104] due to the fall of the regime in Albania and the arrival of immigrants from Albania to Greece. Racism and xenophobia were starkly promoted by the media which placed a great emphasis on the alleged criminality of foreigners. To add to the rising feelings of insecurity was the dispute about the name of Macedonia.[105] As such, the xenophobic stance adopted by the media as well as the mainstream political parties created fertile ground upon which Golden Dawn could (violently) disseminate its own message and agenda. One of the most serious attacks took place in 1998 when the second in charge, Antonis Androutsopoulos, nearly killed a student and seriously wounded two others, all members of a leftist group. After being on the run for several years, he decided to hand himself in and, in 2006, was convicted and sentenced to 12 years in prison,[106] but only remained imprisoned for four and a half years. The case is further discussed below. This occurrence resulted in the party suspending its activities for a while.[107] Unfortunately, the number of violent activities carried out by Golden Dawn, even the known attacks, are so many that it is

---

102 Special Investigation Department: Athens Court of Appeal: Report to the President of the Greek Parliament regarding lifting the immunity of Golden Dawn Members of Parliament, Document Number 305 (19 February 2014) 21.

103 Dimitris Psaras, 'The Black Bible of Golden Dawn: The Documented History and Action of a Nazi Group' ('Η Μαύρη Βίβλος της Χρυσής Αυγής, Ντοκουμέντα από την Ιστορία και τη Δράση Μιας Ναζιστικής Ομάδας') (1st edn. Polis, Athens 2012) 63.

104 Ibid.

105 Ibid.

106 Antonis A. Ellinas, 'The Rise of Golden Dawn: The New Face of the Far Right in Greece' (2013) 18 South European Politics and Society 4, 548.

107 Ibid.

impossible to make reference to all of them in this book. However, some of the most serious known examples of Golden Dawn violence include the killing of Shehzad Luqman, a Pakistani immigrant cycling to work, the murder of anti-fascist musician Pavlos Fyssas and the serious attacks on trade union coalition PAME – All-Workers Militant Front (ΠΑΜΕ – Πανεργατικό Αγωνιστικό Μέτωπο) trade unions and Embarak Abouzid during the attack on a house inhabited by Egyptian fishermen, all discussed hereinafter. As well as individual attacks, and attacks on market stalls,[108] there have been attacks on religious and cultural centres, migrant organisations and homes in which migrants live.[109]

Given the dramatic rise of such violence during the peak of Golden Dawn and the absence of its systematic recording by the state, the National Human Rights Commission, the United Nations High Commissioner for Refugees (UNHCR) in Greece and a number of NGOs set up the Racist Violence Recording Network. However, it does not cover the whole of Greece and has been completely dependent on the will of victims to report such crimes to the Network. As such, any findings are not reflective of the full extent of the situation *vis-à-vis* racist crime in Greece.[110] Further, the Ombudsperson drew up a special report on hate crime in Greece, which included research carried out for 16 months from 1 January 2012 to 30 April 2013. This found that 281 cases[111] of such violence took place in the particular timeframe.[112] In 71 cases, the perpetrators were involved or appeared to be involved with Golden Dawn. Importantly, from January to April 2012, three reports of Golden Dawn violence were made but between May and the end of 2012, 54 such reports were made. Further, in the first four months of 2013, although the number of reports for racist incidents fell, the involvement of Golden

108 Human Rights First, 'We're not Nazis, but…The Rise of Hate Parties in Hungary and Greece and Why America should Care' (August 2014) 91.

109 Council of Europe Commissioner for Human Rights – Report on Greece, CommDH(2013) 6, 3.

110 European Commission against Racism and Intolerance: Report on Greece (24 February 2015) para. 611.

111 Ombudsperson: Special Report: The Phenomenon of Racist Violence in Greece and How it Can be Tackled' (Το Φαινόμενο της Ρατσιστικής Βίας στην Ελλάδα και η Αντιμετώπισή του') (September 2013) 7: The majority of victims were Asian from Pakistan, Bangladesh and Afghanistan and Africans – from Egypt, Morocco and Algeria.

112 Ombudsperson: Special Report: The Phenomenon of Racist Violence in Greece and How it Can be Tackled' (Το Φαινόμενο της Ρατσιστικής Βίας στην Ελλάδα και η Αντιμετώπισή του') (September 2013) 65.

Dawn rose to 46.50% of the incidents.[113] The report's findings have been described in the report as the 'tip of the iceberg'[114] given that the majority of attacks are not reported or are reported and not recorded or recorded without the racist motive.[115] Indicative of this reality is the 2013 statement made by staff members of Doctors of the World in Greece who held that they were receiving one to six victims of racist violence who need medical attention each week.[116]

1.1.3.3 (III) GOLDEN DAWN'S ELECTORAL DEVELOPMENT

Golden Dawn registered as a political party in 1983. From 1994 up until 2010, it remained a marginalised political party with limited electoral success, receiving, for example, 0.11% and 0.07% of the vote in national and European elections respectively.[117] After suspending its activities for a short while following Androutsopoulos' conviction, in its 2007 general assembly it decided to contest the next local, national and European elections.[118] In the 2009 national and European elections it received 0.29% and 0.46% of the vote respectively and no seats in either one.[119] However, in 2010 it saw a rise in its electoral support at a local level, with its leader receiving 5.29 % of the Athens vote.[120] As Michaloliakos noted, 'in 2010 we said we should take over Athens in order to spread the message to the rest of Greece as well. We strategically participated in this election for this reason. We knew we would succeed.'[121] It is important to note that he received particular support in the sixth district of Athens which houses the area of Agios Panteleimonas. As noted, 'the high concentration of immigrants... and the seeming abandonment of the area by the state highlighted the electoral potential.'[122] In fact, the party resorted to anti-immigrant violence in the particular area to gain such support. The great leap forward,

---

113 Ibid. 12.
114 Ibid. 7.
115 Ibid.
116 Council of Europe Commissioner for Human Rights – Report on Greece, CommDH(2013) 6, 3.
117 Antonis A. Ellinas, 'The Rise of Golden Dawn: The New Face of the Far-Right in Greece' (2013) 18 *South European Society and Politics South* 4, 548.
118 Ibid.
119 Ibid.
120 Ibid.
121 Ibid. 549.
122 Ibid.

however, was taken in the national elections of May 2012, in which the party's performance rose to 6.97%, gaining 21 seats out of the 300 in parliament.[123] In the national elections of June 2012 it received 6.92% of the vote and 18 seats in parliament.[124] 462,025 Greeks voted for Golden Dawn during this period, an occurrence which has been described as a 'double electoral earthquake.'[125] Even after the arrest of its leadership, the party managed to maintain its electoral support, gaining 9.8% of the vote in the 2014 European elections, sending three members to the European parliament and coming in third place.[126] In the 2015 national elections of January, its support fell slightly in comparison to the previous national elections, gaining 6.28% of the vote and 17 MPs. However, due to results of other parties, it moved to third place. The slight fall of January 2015 was quickly rectified by September of the same year in which Golden Dawn received 6.99% of the vote and 18 MPs. During the 2019 European parliament election, the party only received 4.88% of the vote, winning two seats, as opposed to 9.4% and three seats in 2014. The major turning point for its electoral performance was the 2019 parliamentary elections where Golden Dawn lost all of its 18 seats in the Greek parliament, receiving only 2.93% of the vote, as opposed to 7.0% in 2015.[127]

In light of the above, it becomes evident that, once Golden Dawn began succeeding electorally, the path it chose to follow was two-sided. On the one hand, it sought to establish an external image of a mainstream political party (albeit which openly rejects the basic tenets of a liberal democracy) which is free of links to National Socialism, whilst on the other, it continued to carry out violent street activities that fall within the framework of a violent subculture movement rather than a political party.[128] Following its electoral success, it decided to demonstrate its legitimacy as a political party rather than as a violent movement by depositing a set of statutes at

123 Electoral Results: <http://ekloges-prev.singularlogic.eu/v2012a/public/index.html#{"cls ":"main","params":{}}> [Accessed 10 September 2021].

124 Electoral Results: <http://ekloges-prev.singularlogic.eu/v2012b/public/#{"cls":"main", "params":{}}> [Accessed 10 September 2021].

125 Dimitris Psaras, 'Golden Dawn before Justice' ('Η Χρυσή Αυγή Μπροστά στη Δικαιοσύνη') (1st edn. Rosa Luxemburg Foundation 2014) 25 'διπλός εκλογικός σεισμός'.

126 Electoral Results: <http://ekloges-prev.singularlogic.eu/may2014/e/public/index.html# {"cls":"main","params":{}}> [Accessed 1- September 2021].

127 For a discussion on this demise look at Georgia Nakou, 'What brought down Golden Dawn' (27 August 2019) MacroPolis: <https://www.macropolis.gr/?i=portal.en.society .8643> [Accessed 10 January 2021].

128 Dimitris Psaras, 'Golden Dawn before Justice' ('Η Χρυσή Αυγή Μπροστά στη Δικαιοσύνη') (1st edn. Rosa Luxemburg Foundation, Berlin 2014) 26.

the Supreme Court, even though it had no obligation to do so.[129] The last but one article of these statutes holds that this document constitutes the first such document, notwithstanding that references had been made to another such document from the first editions of the *Golden Dawn* magazine issued over 20 years ago, as mentioned above. With this move it sought to appear as a legitimate party, with a legitimate constitution.

1.1.3.3 (IV) REASONS FOR GOLDEN DAWN'S RISE

Golden Dawn saw a dramatic rise in a country which had experienced a Nazi invasion in 1941 and a military dictatorship from 1967 to 1974. How was it possible for a nation who had lived through the dire effects of fascism and Nazism to vote Golden Dawn into third place? On one level, this question could be answered by citing the financial crisis. In August 2013, the unemployment rate in Greece reached nearly 28%, more than double the EU average. Unemployment among young people under 25 years old skyrocketed to 62% in June 2013. In a 2013 survey, it was found that 99% of Greeks believed the economy to be in bad shape. This was the highest percentage among the 39 nations included. Moreover, 99% of Greeks believed unemployment to be a very big problem and 94% were concerned about rising prices. Additionally, Greeks did not expect the economic situation in their country to improve. A majority of the Greeks (64%) were pessimistic about the economy's future in the next year and 54% believed their personal situation would be worse over the next 12 months.[130] The first Memorandum of Understanding was signed in 2010 and two followed in 2012 and 2015 respectively. This led to major austerity measures such as spending cuts, tax increases and reforms, moving the country into a great economic depression. As noted in the 2014 country report submitted by Greece to the UN's Human Rights Committee, 'in times of economic crisis, extremist organisations or individuals attempt to exploit the anger or the discontent of some segment of the population to advance their social and political agenda.'[131] Golden Dawn MEP, Ilias Kasidiaris said, 'the Members of Parliament of Syriza have every right

---

129 Ibid. 28.
130 Pew Research Centre, 'The New Sick Man of Europe: The European Union' (13 May 2013) available at: https://www.pewresearch.org/global/2013/05/13/chapter-1-dispirited-over-national-conditions/ [Accessed 26 November 2021].
131 HRC: Consideration of reports submitted by States Parties under article 40 of the Covenant, Greece CCPR/C/GRC/2 (21 February 2014) 32.

to be afraid that the approval of this bailout will conclude with a rise of Golden Dawn ... Golden Dawn will rise because Golden Dawn expresses the proud "no" that the Greek citizens voted for.'[132] Former Minister of Finance, Yiannis Varoufakis noted that 'I cannot see any other possible outcome than the further strengthening of Golden Dawn ... They will inherit the mantle of the anti-austerity drive, tragically.'[133]

Whilst the exploitation of people's insecurities and discontent in such a financially dire period is a reality, the financial crisis itself is not a sufficient reason fully to explain the rise of this violent far-right party. As argued, other European countries, which were also affected by the crisis such as Portugal, Ireland, Spain, Cyprus and Italy did not witness such a rise of the far-right.[134] Instead, as will be demonstrated below, the case of Greece saw the translation of the financial crisis into a simultaneous socio-political crisis, set against the backdrop of a rise in immigration.

The reality is that, apart from the consequences of the financial crisis, the rise of Golden Dawn was facilitated by the interrelated political crisis. Society became frustrated with and lost confidence in the effectiveness of the traditionally dominant political parties, namely *PASOK* and *New Democracy*. For example, good governance indicators between 2003 and 2013 demonstrated that people's trust in the political system declined with perceptions of government stability falling from 61.5% in 2003 to 39.3% in 2013, government effectiveness falling from 75.1% to 67% and people's confidence in judicial impartiality and effectiveness falling from 73.7% to 63.5%.[135] As well as these figures, practical examples exist which demonstrate the people's dismay with the leading parties, such as an 'increase in incidents of public insults against politicians and the disruption of high symbolic public events.'[136] People's disappointment translated into an electoral low for the two major parties. For example, in 2012, *PASOK* and *New Democracy*, which averaged 83.8% of the vote in ten elections between 1981 and 2009, fell to 32% of the vote in the

132 Human Rights First, 'Golden Dawn and the Greek Debt Crisis' (2015) available at: <https://www.humanrightsfirst.org/blog/golden-dawn-and-greek-debt-crisis> [Accessed 20 November 2021].

133 Ibid.

134 As argued, other European countries which were also affected by the crisis such as Portugal, Ireland, Spain, Cyprus and Italy did not witness such a rise of the far-right.

135 Worldwide governance indicators, Greece: <http://info.worldbank.org/governance/wgi/index.aspx#countryReports > [Accessed 1 February 2021].

136 Antonis A. Ellinas, 'The Rise of Golden Dawn: The New Face of the Far Right in Greece' (2013) 18 *South European Politics and Society* 4, 556.

May 2012 election.[137] As such, the fall of the two traditionally dominant parties subsequently made way for the rise of smaller parties. However, by 2019, New Democracy was back in power.

In addition to the above, the rhetoric of Golden Dawn was facilitated by the normalisation of racism occurring on a political and institutional level. In Greece, nationalism is evident in the rhetoric of all parties 'regardless of ideology or other social cleavages.'[138] This foundational setting facilitates the adoption of racist and xenophobic rhetoric as mainstream rhetoric on a political level. As noted by the Council of Europe Commissioner for Human Rights, Greek politicians stigmatise groups such as migrants and the Roma whilst immigration control measures further stigmatise migrants.[139] He argued that this 'reinforces the influence of racist parties such as Golden Dawn, triggers further intolerance and leads to the trivialisation of racism in society.'[140] Examples of such political speech include the reference in 2012 by the prime minister of the time that irregular migrants had 'occupied' certain areas, carrying out 'illegal activities.'[141] In the same year, the Minister of Public Order and Citizen Protection held that because of irregular migration the 'country perishes. Ever since the Dorians' invasion 4000 years ago, never before has the country been subjected to an invasion of these dimensions … this is a bomb on the foundations of the society and the state.'[142] Soon after, on its (now defunct) website, Golden Dawn held that this statement was a 'vindication of the positions of the party.'[143] Note that Golden Dawn now disseminates its ideas predominantly through its YouTube channels. The above statements were made within the framework of the infamous

---

137 Ibid. 544.
138 Sofia Vasilopoulou & Daphne Halikiopoulou, '*The Golden Dawn's Nationalist Solution – Explaining the Rise of the Far-Right in Greece*' (1st edn. Palgrave 2015) 81.
139 Council of Europe Commissioner for Human Rights – Report on Greece, CommDH(2013)6, 1.
140 Ibid. 4.
141 Prime minister's speech to the parliamentary group of New Democracy, 4 November 2012: <http://www.primeminister.gov.gr/2012/11/04/9815> [Accessed 24 February 2021]: «κυρίως, στα κέντρα των πόλεων που είχαν καταληφθεί από λαθρομετανάστες και είχαν παραδοθεί στις παράνομες δραστηριότητές τους».
142 Article in newspaper 'To Vima' (6 August 2012): «λόγω της παράνομης μετανάστευσης χώρα χάνεται...από την εισβολή των Δωριέων, 4000 χρόνια πριν, ποτέ μέχρι σήμερα η χώρα δεν έχει υποστεί μια εισβολή τέτοιων διαστάσεων... αυτό είναι μία βόμβα στα θεμέλια της κοινωνίας και του κράτους».
143 Publication on Golden Dawn's website on 14 July 2012: <http://www.xryshaygh.com/>: «δικαίωση των θέσεων μας» Note the website is no longer functioning.

Xenios-Zeus[144] operation, which started in July 2012 during which 4,500 police officers, using racial profiling as their key tool, entered the centre of Athens, making thousands of arrests as a means of cracking down on irregular migration. Golden Dawn acted concurrently with this mission, with violent attacks happening all over the country.[145]

Thus, racist rhetoric is not confined to the political discourse of the far-right and racist activities are institutionalised, as illustrated in the Xenios-Zeus operation. This normalisation of racism allowed for the speech and activities of Golden Dawn to appear more acceptable, both by society and its institutions. In addition to this, on a societal level, rising sentiments of racism and xenophobia facilitated the rise of Golden Dawn with such sentiments already having commenced in the 1990s. From the beginning of the 1990s, the Eurobarometer demonstrated a drastic change in the sentiments of Greek society towards foreigners and especially migrants. Within four years, from 1991 to 1994, Greece moved from the last place to the first place in relation to anti-immigrant sentiments. At the same time, Golden Dawn's systematic attacks against political opponents and, in turn, against migrants commenced. In fact, the Human Rights Committee placed its discussion on the rise of the far-right in Greece against the backdrop of the unprecedented rise in irregular migration.[146] In sum, the racist and xenophobic character of Golden Dawn was facilitated by the racism and xenophobia that existed on both an institutional and societal level which at first tolerated and, in terms of the electorate, endorsed it in relatively large numbers.

1.1.3.3 (V) GOLDEN DAWN'S IMPUNITY: A FACILITATING FACTOR OF ITS RISE

The above section sought to extrapolate on the conditions which created a fertile ground upon which Golden Dawn managed to gain electoral support. However, when considering this group's development, it is also significant to take into account how and why it was able to carry out violent activities without the interference of the state for a long period of time. There are several serious allegations that Golden Dawn infiltrated the police force and, in this way, managed to ensure impunity for its

---

144 This is an ironic name since Xenios Zeus denotes hospitality.
145 Amnesty International: 'Imperium in Imperio: Culture of Bad Treatment and Impunity in the Greek police' (2014) <https://www.amnesty.gr/news/ektheseis/article/20068/kratos-en-kratei-koyltoyra-kakometaheirisis-kai-atimorisias-stin> [Accessed 4 October 2021].
146 HRC Concluding Observations: Greece (3 December 2015) CCPR/C/GRC/CO/2, 31.

violent activities.[147] For example, in Athens polling stations, where members of the Greek police along with other Greek citizens voted during the 2012 national elections, Golden Dawn percentages were far above the national average, ranging from 17.2% to 23.04%. It is estimated that 'more than 50% of the police officials in these polling stations voted for Golden Dawn.'[148] As well as voting for this party, video footage has emerged which shows police officers standing by as Golden Dawn members threw stones at opposition groups.[149] In light of these realities, the Ombudsperson spoke of the 'passive stance' taken by the police towards hate crime incidents.[150] In fact, following the arrests of Golden Dawn MPs and members, the Minister of Public Order instructed the Chief of Police and the Director of Internal Affairs to investigate the allegation of police involvement and/or the facilitation of Golden Dawn's violent activities. Although eight senior officials were suspended pending the investigation, in 2014 the Director held that 15 police officers had been arrested, ten of whom were found to be 'directly or indirectly linked to the criminal activities of Golden Dawn.'[151] He concluded, however, that, following the investigation and although 'extremist behaviour'[152] had been identified in 203 policemen/women, 'there was no evidence of cells or factions of para-constitutional forces in the Greek police.'[153] This has been deemed not to be reflective of the real situation with the

---

147 Human Rights First, 'We're not Nazis, but…The Rise of Hate Parties in Hungary and Greece and Why America should Care' (August 2014) 26.

148 Council of Europe Commissioner for Human Rights – Report on Greece, CommDH(2013)6, 122.

149 Human Rights First, 'We're not Nazis, but…The Rise of Hate Parties in Hungary and Greece and Why America should Care' (August 2014) 100.

150 Ombudsperson: Special Report: The Phenomenon of Racist Violence in Greece and How it Can be Tackled' (Το Φαινόμενο της Ρατσιστικής Βίας στην Ελλάδα και η Αντιμετώπισή του') (September 2013) 66.

151 30 October 2013: Press conference of the Director of Internal Affairs (of the Police) Panagiotis Stathis following the investigation of accusations of police and Golden Dawn cooperation. Cited in Human Rights First, 'We're not Nazis, but…The Rise of Hate Parties in Hungary and Greece and Why America should Care' (August 2014) 101.

152 30 October 2013: Press conference of the Director of Internal Affairs (of the Police) Panagiotis Stathis following the investigation of accusations of police and Golden Dawn cooperation: «Ακραίες συμπεριφορές από 203 αστυνομικούς σε Άμεση Δράση, Αλλοδαπών, Αθήνα, Πειραιά και Δυτική Αττική».

153 30 October 2013: Press conference of the Director of Internal Affairs (of the Police) Panagiotis Stathis following the investigation of accusations of police and Golden Dawn cooperation: «δεν διαπιστώνει συγκρότηση πυρήνων ή φραξιών ή παρασυνταγματικών πόλων στην Ελληνική Αστυνομία».

link between the police and Golden Dawn being reiterated by several national and international organisations such as Amnesty International.[154] The link between Golden Dawn and the general inertia of the police to act in cases involving groups such as migrants or Roma has deeply hampered the victims' access to justice due to a lack of immediate investigatory activities such as going to the crime scene, finding and examining witnesses and collecting material, a reality which has contributed to the impunity of Golden Dawn.[155] As well as the police, other institutions have been deemed to have facilitated the implementation of Golden Dawn's objectives with there existing an 'outrageous cover-up of Golden Dawn's actions by the Greek Police, state mechanism and the ministries.'[156] It must be noted that only an estimate of 1% to 2% of Golden Dawn attacks over the past 20 years have reached the courts,[157] demonstrating a failure of the state to crack down on the violent actions of this party.

In relation to the judiciary, for the cases that have eventually reached the courts, the circumstances are no better in that racist motives of Golden Dawn perpetrators were seldom found. As noted by one lawyer, 'the impunity of the organisation has to do not only with the police but also with the judiciary.'[158] The impunity could be based on lack of knowledge on relevant legal provisions, as noted by the Council of Europe Commissioner for Human Rights,[159] but could also stem from bias. According to a study conducted in 2008 which considered records of the Criminal Appeals Court in Athens, the criminal treatment of persons differentiates according to racial criteria, with the key finding of the research being that migrants, especially migrant men aged 35 to 50 who

---

154 Amnesty International: 'Imperium in Imperio: Culture of Bad Treatment and Impunity in the Greek Police' (2014):<https://www.amnesty.gr/news/ektheseis/article/20068/kratos -en-kratei-koyltoyra-kakometaheirisis-kai-atimorisias-stin> [Accessed 1 November 2021].

155 Dimitris Psaras, 'The Black Bible of Golden Dawn: The Documented History of a Nazi Group' ('Η Μαύρη Βίβλος της Χρυσής Αυγής, Ντοκουμέντα από την Ιστορία και τη Δράση μιας Ναζιστικής Ομάδας) (1st edn. Polis, Athens 2012) 166.

156 Attorneys of the Civil Action: Memo of the Civil Action of the Anti-Fascist Movement for the Trial of Golden Dawn (Υπόμνημα της Πολιτικής Αγωγής του Αντιφασιστικού Κινήματος για τη Δίκη της Χρυσής Αυγής) (1st edn.Marxist Bookshop, Athens 2015) 6.

157 Katerina Toidou & Giorgos Pittas, 'Golden Dawn's File – Neo Nazi Crimes and How to Stop them' ('Φάκελος Χρυσή Αυγή – τα Εγκλήματα των Νεοναζί και πώς να τους Σταματήσουμε') (1st edn. Marxist Bookshop, Athens 2013) 45.

158 Ibid. 46.

159 Council of Europe Commissioner for Human Rights – Report on Greece, CommDH(2013) 6, 9.

are labourers, receive unequal treatment when it comes to sentencing in comparison to Greeks.[160] Although this finding considered the position of foreigners when defendants in criminal trials, it nevertheless demonstrates a tendency of racism and xenophobia within part of the judiciary, which has the potential to taint significantly the outcome of trials that involve potential racist motives. A prejudicial and/or indifferent stance to foreigners was also reflected on an executive level in 2012. More particularly, in receiving a report by the National Human Rights Committee, which highlighted the issue of racist violence, a former Cabinet Secretary stated that 'we are not interested in the human rights of foreigners.'[161]

The Greek state proved to be unwilling to take an active stance against the rhetoric and violence of Golden Dawn up until the moment that Pavlos Fyssas was murdered by a Golden Dawn member after a hit squad appeared at the café where he was sitting with his friends and subsequently chased him in the streets. This is notwithstanding that the state had been faced with several cases before that of Fyssas in which it was made aware of Golden Dawn and its activities. One of the most significant demonstrations of the state's knowledge of the intentions and means of the functioning of Golden Dawn was the case of Antonis Androutsopoulos.[162] Androutsopoulos (known as 'Periandros')[163] was found guilty of attacks that took place in 1998 against three (leftists), Dimitris Kousouris, Ilias Fotiadis and Ioannis Karampatsolis, who were participating in a protest. In its judgement, the court underlined that he had acted along with other people who were all members of Golden Dawn and that they had decided to kill Dimitris Kousouris. Androutsopoulos and his accomplices had managed 'with great savagery and barbarianism to cause multiple wounds to his head and body.'[164] As well as acknowledging the affiliation with Golden Dawn, the court described the relationship between the party and the hit squads and confirmed that the violent activities occurred within the framework of the party rather than on an individual basis.[165] Further, the court held that the group had the capacity to attempt

---

160 Research conducted by Vasilis Karidis (Professor of Criminology and Assistant to the Ombudsperson) 2008.

161 UNHCR, Marcus Walker & Marianna Kakaounaki: 'Greece Struggles to Outlaw its Golden Dawn Fascist Party' (2013).

162 Case161,162,163/2009 which was upheld by Case 11167/2010 of the Supreme Court.

163 In ancient Greek history, Periandros (or Periander in English) was the Second Tyrant of the Cypselid dynasty that ruled over ancient Corinth.

164 Case 161, 162, 163/2009.

165 Ibid.

to kill those it considers enemies of its ideology, as was the case with Kousouris.[166] Even though the defendant sought to challenge this point at the Supreme Court, by holding that he had been convicted because he was a member of a group which differed ideologically to that of the victim, the court rejected this argument and found homicidal intent.[167] The court passed judgement in 2009, sentencing him to 21 years in prison whilst, in 2010, the Appellant Court lowered his sentence to 12 years. Although this case was briefly discussed in parliament and even though the court found that the party's attacks were organised with murderous intentions and driven by its ideology, no steps were taken as they were following the murder of Pavlos Fyssas. Here, it is important to underline that during the attack, the electoral success of Golden Dawn was at a bare minimum. Also, as noted above, Golden Dawn suspended its activities for a short while following Androutsopoulos conviction.

There are other cases where the courts have made reference to perpetrators' links with Golden Dawn. For example, in case 30841A/2011,[168] the court held that the two people who were charged with attempted homicide against two others claimed to be members of Golden Dawn.[169] In 4020/2006,[170] the court held that in 2001, the perpetrator participated in a public assembly whose participants carried out violent activities against persons and properties. 'Particularly, he participated in the group Golden Dawn which was concentrated outside the main entrance of the courthouse and attacked police forces and members of the *Socialist Labour Party*, throwing yogurts and sharp objects and causing damages to parked cars.'[171] It must be noted that the systematic reaction of Golden Dawn's leadership to any reference to the party's involvement in crimes was to argue that their members had not been part of the particular occurrence

---

166 *Attorneys of the Civil Action: Memo of the Civil Action of the Anti-Fascist Movement for the Trial of Golden Dawn (Υπόμνημα της Πολιτικής Αγωγής του Αντιφασιστικού Κινήματος για τη Δίκη της Χρυσής Αυγής)* (1st edn. Marxist Bookshop 2015) 23.

167 Case 1607/2010.

168 Another case in which Golden Dawn was referred to and its violent activities was case 4775/2009.

169 Case 30841A/2011.

170 Case 4020/2006.

171 Dimitris Psaras, *'The Black Bible of Golden Dawn: The Documented History of a Nazi Group'* (Ή Μαύρη Βίβλος της Χρυσής Αυγής, Ντοκουμέντα από την Ιστορία και τη Δράση μιας Ναζιστικής Ομάδας) (1st edn. Polis, Athens 2012) 170.

and attributing the reference to the party as a plot of its political opponents, seeking to appear as victims of the system.[172] Furthermore, the parliament was also confronted with the party's violence and the issue of lifting the immunity of some of its MPs for cases that took place in 2007 and 2012. Parliament lifted the parliamentary immunity of party spokesperson, Ilias Kasidiaris, charged with taking part in a robbery and causing bodily harm in 2007.[173] In 2012, parliament lifted the immunity of three Golden Dawn MPs so that the court could proceed with the charges of falsification of authority and destruction of foreign property after they participated in destroying the stalls owned by migrant street vendors and carried out identification/documentation checks on such persons.[174]

As such, Golden Dawn enjoyed a large degree of impunity due to the stances adopted by the different organs of the state, either due to their indifference to the issue and/or due to their own prejudicial approaches to some of the groups which Golden Dawn targeted but also due to the direct link between Golden Dawn's activities and the police. This state of impunity allowed Golden Dawn to sow its violent seeds and develop itself into a criminal organisation, a status which it was finally found to hold.

In light of the above, it becomes clear that the state and its institutions were aware of the violent actions of Golden Dawn, its hit squad tactics, its homicidal intent in certain cases and the link between such intent and its ideology. Further, parliament was confronted with the involvement of some of the party's MPs in violent activities against persons and property. Notwithstanding this, the state institutions never took a sincere and effective stance on cracking down on its leadership but, rather, let Golden Dawn flourish and extend its violence and, at times, homicidal intent towards their targets. Whilst the sanctity of political parties, as discussed later on, is a major characteristic of the Greek legal order, the criminal law framework could have been invoked to shut down the actions of Golden Dawn's criminal nature. This only happened when Pavlos Fyssas was murdered.

172 Dimitris Psaras, 'Golden Dawn before Justice' (Η Χρυσή Αυγή Μπροστά στη Δικαιοσύνη') (1st edn. Rosa Luxemburg Foundation, Berlin 2014) 13.

173 Council of Europe Commissioner for Human Rights – Report on Greece, CommDH (2013) 6, 3.

174 European Network of Legal Experts in the Non-Discrimination Field, Athanasios Theodoridis, 'Report on Measures to Combat Discrimination – Directives 2000/43/EC and 2000/78/EC – Country Report 2013 – State of affairs up to 1st January 2014' 134, Council of Europe Commissioner for Human Rights – Report on Greece, CommDH(2013) 6, 3.

1.1.3.3 (VI) THE MURDER OF PAVLOS FYSSAS – THE TURNING POINT

For several years, Golden Dawn acted violently against migrants, political opponents and other groups its considered not to belong to its world theories and belief system, without fear of any serious repercussions from the state and its institutions. This reality altered almost immediately following the murder of Pavlos Fyssas, an ethnic Greek anti-fascist musician, on the evening of 17 (towards 18) September 2013 by Georgios Roupakias, a member of the party's council in the area of Nikea, with the aid of a hit squad who had chased Fyssas from a café he was in through the streets.[175] ECRI underlined that the 'fact that hundreds of attacks against foreigners, including several killings, had not resulted in any steps against this organisation but that this required the death of a Greek is, in itself, worrying.'[176] It must be noted that just a few months earlier, the murder of Pakistani immigrant, Shehzad Luqman, by Golden Dawn members had not led to an equivalent response by the authorities. It was only after the murder of an ethnic Greek that Greece witnessed 'an unprecedented mobilization of law enforcement mechanisms'[177] which resulted in the arrest and prosecution of the leadership and some members of the party. Either way, for some, 'this long delay in initiating prosecution was a sign that the judiciary or the government ... had thus far actively protected Golden Dawn out of ideological sympathy.'[178] Whilst the judiciary seldom found racist motives to drive Golden Dawn criminality, and whilst other branches of the government were aware of this criminality as discussed above, this statement must be read with caution given the constitutional limitations on the prohibition of political parties. The very nature of Golden Dawn's functioning as a political party and a criminal group complicated its crack down since the constitutional protection of political parties is strict. Whilst this by no means excuses the delay in the use of the Criminal Code kickstarted by the executive branch following Fyssas's murder, it does contribute to the understanding of the treatment of Golden Dawn by the state over time. In relation to the judiciary, it is

---

175 *Attorneys of the Civil Action: Memo of the Civil Action of the Anti-Fascist Movement for the Trial of Golden Dawn (Υπόμνημα της Πολιτικής Αγωγής του Αντιφασιστικού Κινήματος για τη Δίκη της Χρυσής Αυγής)* (1st edn. Marxist Bookshop, Athens 2015) 82.

176 European Commission against Racism and Intolerance: Report on Greece (24 February 2021) para. 73.

177 Heinrich Böll Stiftung, 'Racism and Discrimination in Greece Today' (Ρατσισμός και Διακρίσεις στην Ελλάδα Σήμερα') (2014) 8.

178 Anthoula Malkopoulou, 'Greece: A Procedural Defense of Democracy against the Golden Dawn' (2021) 17 *European Constitutional Law Review* 191.

highlighted that the public prosecutors who belong to the judicial branch of the Greek government had to pay attention to the nature and sanctity of political parties. At the same time, the judiciary 'whose esprit des corps demanded a double devotion to … the constitution and to criminal law' was an intricately complex situation. Executive support in the form of a communication sent by the Minister of Public Order and Protection of Citizens to the Supreme Court's Prosecutor regarding Golden Dawn's activities following Fyssas's murder was, therefore, a 'green light' for the public prosecutor's offices to proceed and this would 'not be interpreted as undue political interference by Supreme Court judges.'[179]

A significant consequence of Golden Dawn's trial has been underlined by the Racist Violence Recording Network which found a significant drop in hate crime following the mass arrests of Golden Dawn members and leaders. More particularly, it recorded 18 incidents for the period between October and December 2013 whilst the average number of the previous three-month period came to 50 incidents.[180] Whilst a positive impact of the arrest of Golden Dawn members, the above finding also reflects the damaging consequences of the fact that the Greek state was much too slow to take measures against its criminality.[181] Moreover, the Network concluded that the above finding demonstrates that such crime was perpetuated by the infamous hit squads of the party.[182] The Head of Doctors of the World in Greece noted that post-2013, due to the fact that the hit squads no longer enjoyed the safety net of impunity, there has been a tendency to resort to other measures such as threatening and humiliating their target groups.[183]

Fyssas's murder has also affected the way in which one particularly serious racist crime has been dealt with, namely, the case of the Egyptian fishermen in Piraeus. In 2012, a Golden Dawn hit squad, made up of at least 20 persons, attempted to enter the house resided in by Egyptian fishermen. They did not manage to break the metal door and so the three persons inside the home managed to escape the attack. However, the hit squad went to the roof where Embarak Abouzid was sleeping. They attacked him with metal rods and wooden bats and seriously injured him

179 Ibid.
180 Racist Violence Recording Network Annual Report 2013: <http://rvrn.org/wp-content /uploads/2014/04/Report2013_EN.pdf> 5 [Accessed 10 February 2021].
181 Ibid.
182 Ibid.
183 Human Rights First, 'We're not Nazis, but…The Rise of Hate Parties in Hungary and Greece and Why America should Care' (August 2014) 94.

on his head and face as well as on his chest.[184] The Prosecutor of Piraeus Magistrates Court chose to prosecute the defendants for grievous bodily harm with intent and, although the defendants had been recognised by the brothers of the victim, they were set free with some restrictions whilst, importantly, no examination of the role of Golden Dawn was incorporated in the investigation or subsequent prosecution. It was only following the murder of Fyssas and the submittal of this case to the investigators (as well as others), for the purposes of demonstrating the criminal activities of Golden Dawn, that there was a supplementary prosecution, incorporating the crime of attempted homicide.[185]

Lastly, Golden Dawn's significant electoral drop (2019) discussed above can reasonably be positively correlated with the trial, particularly as it moved to a close.

1.1.3.3 (VII) GOLDEN DAWN'S TRIAL

From the onset, it must be highlighted that Golden Dawn's trial was a criminal one and not a political one. The prosecution of the party occurred within the framework of Greece's Criminal Code given the party's functioning as a criminal organisation. Following Fyssas's murder, the Minister of Public Order and Protection of Citizens sent a document to the Supreme Court's Prosecutor regarding the activities of Golden Dawn's MPs. This document noted that their activities

> are not isolated incidents ... they undermine the rule of law, offend human rights and human dignity, endanger public order and the internal security of the country, go against the democratic tradition and legal culture of the country as well as its obligations as they emanate from international and European human rights law.[186]

The document requested the Public Prosecutor to investigate Golden Dawn for acting as a criminal organisation on the basis of a list of 32 cases annexed to the document.[187] Based on this, and following the

---

184 Prosecutor's Recommendation to the Appeals Council regarding the Prosecution of Golden Dawn members and Members of Parliament (15 October 2014) 75.

185 Civil Action (Case files ABM Φ2013/3990, ABM Φ2012/979 and 979A) 14.

186 Case 4003/173/315661/19-902913.

187 Anthoula Malkopoulou, 'Greece: A Procedural Defense of Democracy against the Golden Dawn' (2021) 17 *European Constitutional Law Review* 190.

instructions of the Supreme Court's Prosecutor, a preliminary investigation was conducted by the Supreme Court for the purposes of determining whether crimes had been conducted by supporters and members of the political party, particularly those related to leading or participating in a criminal organisation.[188] This investigation found that there were sufficient indications to justify the prosecution of the members/MPs of this organisation, particularly in relation to Article 187 of the Criminal Code.[189] Although this article will be discussed below, for purposes of clarity, reference will be made here to the key points found therein. Article 187(1) of the Criminal Code punishes whoever establishes or participates in a criminal organisation with imprisonment of up to ten years. The leader of such an organisation receives a prison sentence of at least ten years.[190] The article holds that a criminal organisation is an entity which includes three or more members that aims to commit an array of offences including, *inter alia*, homicide with intent, grievous bodily harm, arson and kidnapping.[191] Following the preliminary investigation of the Supreme Court, two investigative judges were appointed to conduct a pre-trial investigation for the purposes of requesting the parliament to lift the immunity of Golden Dawn MPs, as set out by Article 62 of the constitution.[192] At the same time as the above procedure for lifting the immunity of the MPs, an officer was appointed the task of investigating the crimes committed by members of the party including Pavlos Fyssas's murder,[193] the attacks against PAME – All-Workers Militant Front (ΠΑΜΕ - Πανεργατικό Αγωνιστικό Μέτωπο, ΠΑΜΕ)[194] and against the Egyptian fisherman with victim Embarak Abouzid.[195] Subsequently, a competent Prosecutor made a recommendation to the Appeals Council (Συμβούλιο Εφετών)[196] based on which the Council prosecuted all parliamentary members and other members of the party for offences such as those related to a criminal organisation and/or homicide. In total, this case involved 69 party officials and members, including the entire

---

188 Case 413 a/28-9-2013.
189 Case 413 a/28-9-2013.
190 Article 187(3) Criminal Code.
191 Article 187 Criminal Code.
192 Case 490/29-9-2013.
193 Case 618/18-9-2013.
194 Case 625/27-9-2013.
195 Case 39/13-6/2012.
196 Article 187 of the Criminal Code provides that it is the Appeals Council which has the role of prosecuting persons for violations of this article.

parliamentary group from the 2012 national elections. All the known criminal activities conducted by Golden Dawn since 2008 are described in the 1,109-page decree.

Three days after Fyssas's murder, a preliminary investigation was ordered which led to their arrest and detention. On 5 February 2015, official charges were filed. This followed a recommendation by the Public Prosecutor and Judicial Council that Golden Dawn leaders and members should stand trial for violating Article 187 of the Greek Criminal Code which prohibits leading and participating in a criminal organisation. In the case against Golden Dawn, the prosecution demonstrated that Golden Dawn is a criminal organisation and that its leadership and members are guilty of leading and/or participating in a criminal organisation, as prohibited by Article 187 of the Criminal Code. As noted in the Prosecutor's recommendation, none of the party's MPs can argue 'convincingly that he/she was unaware of the party's criminal activities, which systematically and for a long period of time were being committed by and for the party.'[197] It is through this approach that it prosecuted Golden Dawn's members and MPs. The victims of Golden Dawn's crimes and/or their relatives were part of the proceedings as a civil party in three cases, namely, the murder of Palos Fyssas, and the attacks on the Egyptian Fishermen and PAME unionists. The prosecution sought to demonstrate that Golden Dawn consisted of about one thousand central cadres and about three to four hundred junior members, divided into cells of four or five members in all parts of Greece.

Six MPs including the leader Michaloliakos and the party's 'spokesperson' Kasidiaris received prison sentences of over 13 years for leading a criminal organisation and one (Matheopoulos) received a sentence of ten years. The rest of the MPs received prison sentences between five and seven years for participating in a criminal organisation. Members (not MPs) charged with participating in a criminal organisation received prison sentences ranging from one to seven years, including, in some cases, a fine. For those involved in Fyssas's murder, the case of the Egyptian fishermen and the case of PAME, sentences between three and

197 Prosecutor's Recommendation to the Appeals Council regarding the Prosecution of Golden Dawn members and members of parliament (15 October 2014) 110: 'Ουδείς εκ των Βουλευτών του ως άνω πολιτικού κόμματος, είναι σε θέση να ισχυριστεί ευπροσώπως και με πειστικότητα ότι ήταν ανυποψίαστος για τις εγκληματικές πράξεις, οι οποίες εξακολουθητικά και επί μακρό χρονικό διάστημα διαπράττονταν εξ ονόματος και για λογαριασμό του κόμματος στο οποίο ανήκει.

ten years were handed down as well as a life sentence for Fyssas's assassin.[198] Excluding Fyssas's murderer, the prison sentences of lay members and MPs amounted to more than 500 years in prison time.[199] In terms of pre-trial detention, Greek law provides this can occur for a time period of up to 18 months and, since this time frame had expired, all defendants were released with different forms of restrictions. For example, Roupakias, the murderer of Pavlos Fyssas, was under house arrest whereas the leader of Golden Dawn had to appear at a police station three times per month.[200] The trial, which began in April 2015 and ended in October 2020, was described as 'the biggest trial of fascist criminality since Nuremberg.'[201] After the verdict of October 2020, 39 of the convicted persons went to jail and 18 more were placed on remand, while the victims have appealed for stricter sentences. One of the convicted leaders and party cadres, Christos Pappas, was on the run for a while. There was also a delay with the arrest of Ioannis Lagos, an elected Member of the European Parliament who had his immunity lifted by the European Parliament and was subsequently arrested on 27 April 2020. In October 2021, Patelis who was imprisoned for ten years was released on the grounds of his child's psychological issues.

As such, following Fyssas's murder, the state mobilised itself, for the first time, against Golden Dawn by looking at it through the lens of a criminal organisation, thereby attaching criminal responsibility to its leadership and members. It also prompted the police to conduct an investigation into its own members and their links to Golden Dawn, albeit with questionable results. However, as underlined at the start of this section, the trial was a criminal one, not a political one. Translating the criminal conviction of the party's leadership and members to dissolution of Golden Dawn as a political party 'has turned out to be a legal puzzle.'[202]

---

198 For a full list of sentences please visit: < https://www.naftemporiki.gr/story/1646377/diki
-xrusis-augis-oi-poines-olon-ton-katadikasthenton> [Accessed 30 April 2021].

199 For a full list of sentences visit: < https://www.in.gr/2020/10/14/greece/xrysi-aygi
-analytika-oi-poines-pou-epivlithikan-se-ola-ta-meli-tis-egklimatikis-organosis-lista/>
[Accessed 30 June 2021].

200 Case 1247/2015.

201 Will Horner, 'What "the Biggest Trial of Fascist Criminality Since Nuremberg" Means
for the Future of Greece' OpenDemocracy (17 November 2016) available at: https://www
.opendemocracy.net/en/can-europe-make-it/what-biggest-trial-of-fascist-criminality
-since-nuremberg-means-for-f/ [Accessed 28 November 2021].

202 Anthoula Malkopoulou, 'Greece: A Procedural Defense of Democracy against the Golden
Dawn' (2021) 17 European Constitutional Law Review 199.

Until 2019, Articles 59–61 of the Criminal Code provided for the loss of political rights for up to ten years following a conviction. However, this was amended, with the new law stipulating that such a loss can occur if the crime led to a 'serious breach of duty' with no loss of political rights linked to off duty criminal activity. Following the trial, there were recommendations that this should be amended. SYRIZA argued for a loss of electoral rights for life, the Communist Party of Greece for a loss of elected positions and political rights and KINAL – Movement for Change (KIN.ΑΛ. – Κίνημα Αλλαγής) for the prohibition of standing for elections. New Democracy (governing) said that the election law would be amended but that this would occur in line with the constitution and that loss of rights would only occur after a final, non-revocable decision.[203] Here, it must be highlighted that according to Article 51 of the constitution, the law 'cannot abridge the right to vote except in cases where a minimum age has not been attained or in cases of legal incapacity or as a result of irrevocable criminal conviction for certain felonies.' The amendment to the electoral law presented to parliament and passed in June 2021 removed Golden Dawn members' right to vote while they are incarcerated, removed their right to be elected as leaders of a political party but maintained the right to be candidates in a party insofar as the leader of the party is not convicted. So, for example, Ilias Kasidiris cannot stand as a candidate for the party Greeks for the Nation – Έλληνες για την Πατρίδα, which he founded and leads. The right to be elected cannot be completely ceased since their conviction is not yet irrevocable.

1.1.3.3 (VIII) THE FAR-RIGHT IN GREECE: CONCLUDING COMMENTS

The post-Junta far-right in Greece has been dominated by one extremist and violent group, Golden Dawn, with characteristics of a violent subculture movement (albeit strictly organised and disciplined) and the legal status of a registered political party, contesting elections and participating in the national and European parliaments. Although other parties came and went, with some, such as LAOS, demonstrating more extended success than others, such successes were short-lived. Golden Dawn, on the other hand, remained on the subculture/street scene from the time of its inception and on the political scene from 2012 until 2019. Its street presence fell dramatically following the arrest of leaders/members. Along

203 Ibid. 200.

with parliamentary seats which have contributed to the rise in hate speech and xenophobic and racist polices and rhetoric on a political level, this party dramatically deteriorated the daily existence, predominantly of migrants, but also of other groups such as ethnic minorities, through hate speech and hate crimes against them. This party's rhetoric and activities went unfettered for a long period of time, up until the point that one of its members murdered Pavlos Fyssas. Only at that point did the tables turn and did the state and its institutions decide to use the law against it. Centrifugal in understanding the treatment of Golden Dawn by the state is the particular sanctity provided to political parties granted by the Greek constitution discussed further down. Whilst this book examines the relevant constitutional provision, placing it within a theoretical and historical context, the author emphatically argues that the Criminal Code, which could be and was ultimately used against the individuals who made up Golden Dawn, was relied on too late, thereby allowing Golden Dawn to spur fear and violence against minorities and political opponents.

1.1.4 Definitional Framework

1.1.4.1 Racial and Religious Groups

Race is not defined in national legislation or case law, as is the case with, amongst others, international documents. There is no definition of religion but an understanding of what is deemed to fall in the framework of religion is facilitated in comparison to race, given that religion is partly described, although not defined, in Article 13 of the constitution. This article holds that 'all known religions shall be free.'[204] However, there is no further discussion in relevant case law or policy regarding the religions which are considered to be known. It has been argued that the constitution 'protects publicly known religions but not mystical and secret practices or dogmas.'[205] This could denote that the state will accept what it considers to be mainstream religions and probably be hostile to sects. The only clear indication is that the Christian Eastern Orthodox Church does not fall within the ambit of 'known religions' but, rather is referred to as the 'dominant religion' in Article 3 of the constitution. Further in Article 198(2) of the Criminal Code on

---

204 'Κάθε γνωστή θρησκεία είναι ελεύθερη'.
205 European Network of Legal Experts in the Non-Discrimination Field, Athanasios Theodoridis, 'Report on Measures to Combat Discrimination – Directives 2000/43/EC and 2000/78/EC – Country Report 2013 – State of affairs up to 1st January 2014' 22.

blasphemy, reference is made to the prohibition of blasphemy insofar as this is directed either to the dominant religion or 'another religion tolerated in Greece.' However, there is no extrapolation in the legislation, case law or policy providing an understanding of which religions are considered tolerated and not tolerated in Greece. There exist no definitions of the terms racial groups and religious groups in national legislation, case law or policy.

1.1.4.2 Public Incitement of Violence and Hatred and Prohibition of Revisionism – A Substitute for Hate Speech?

Greek legislation offers no definition of hate speech but, instead, the provision relating to inciting violence, hatred and discrimination must be relied upon when seeking to tackle this phenomenon. Greece also provides for a prohibition of publicly condoning, trivialising or maliciously denying the existence or severity of certain international crimes. The first element, namely inciting violence, hatred and discrimination, is defined by Article 1 of Law 972/1979 as amended by Law 4285/2014. It punishes any person who

> intends, publicly or orally or through the press, through the internet or in any other way or manner, to incite, promote, arouse or promote actions which may cause discrimination, hatred or violence against a person or group of persons due to their race, religion, genealogical origins, ethnic or racial origin, sexual orientation, gender identity or disability, in a way which poses a danger to public order or constitutes a threat to the life, liberty or physical integrity of the above persons.

However, no definition of the majority of terms contained in the above articles is provided for either in legislation, case law or policy. In fact, the only terms relevant to the above section which are given some definition, albeit not in the law under consideration, are those of discrimination and racial discrimination, discussed further on. Part two of the same article refers to speech which seeks to result in property damage insofar as such property is utilised by the above-mentioned groups, only if such actions cause damage to public order. As such, this article can be seen, to an extent, as a substitute for a definition of hate speech but the effects of the speech must either result in public harm or serious individual harm. Therefore, Greece opted to take the more speech-protective approach offered by the Framework Decision which holds, amongst other things, that for offences concerning racism and xeno-phobia, states may choose to punish conduct which is likely to disturb public order. In the event of damage to property as harm, there must be a necessary correlation to the infliction of public disorder. Further, Greece chose to incorporate the requirement of 'threatening,' an option provided for by Article 12 of the Framework Decision, but did not include the other optional provisions, namely that of conduct which is abusive or insulting and depicts a less severe case in comparison to the situation of threatening conduct. As per the Framework Decision and also the old law, the perpetrators must intend for such harm to be the result of his/her/their speech and actions. It must be noted that the requirements regarding public order or serious individual harm were not a necessity in the old law and, as such, the 2014 amendments restricted the conceptualisation of hateful expression. Further, the old law incorporated offensive speech as prohibited speech in Article 2, something which is not incorporated in the amended law. In addition, following the incorporation of the Framework Decision, Greek law also contains another form of hate speech in Article 2. More particularly, this article punishes whoever publicly, orally or through the press or the internet or through any other means condones, trivialises or maliciously denies the existence or the severity of crimes of genocide, war crimes, crimes against humanity, the Holocaust and Nazi crimes which have been recognised by international courts or the Greek parliament and this behaviour is directed against a group of persons determined by their race, colour, religion, descent, racial or ethnic group, sexual orientation, gender identity or disability, insofar as such behaviour is manifested in a way which can incite violence or hatred or is of a threatening or abusive character against such a group or a member of such a group. In relation to the parliament's role in recognising such crimes, this has been deemed unconstitutional in the case against historian Heinz Richter discussed below. Thus, condoning, trivialising or denying the severity or existence of international crimes, such as the Holocaust, is punishable. However, such punishment is dependent on certain factors constituting safety nets for freedom of expression such as the necessity of intention on the part of the perpetrator and the establishment of a link between the speech and the incitement to violence or hatred. In relation to religion, it must be noted that the Greek Criminal Code provides for the offence of blasphemy. The relevant provision is Article 198(2) therein, which holds that anyone who publicly and maliciously reviles the Eastern Orthodox Church of Jesus Christ or another religion tolerated in Greece is punished with imprisonment of up to two years.

This provision has not been used to prosecute any religiously hateful/ offensive speech uttered by the far-right movement.

1.1.4.3 Racial and Religious Aggravation and Hate Crime: Two in One

Before amendments brought about by Law 4285/2014, the Greek Penal Code contained Article 79(3) which held, amongst other things, that committing an act out of hate based on ethnic, racial, religious hate or hate due to the descent of the victim constitutes an aggravating circumstance. However, Law 4285/2014 abolished the part of Article 79(3) on such aggravation and introduced Article 81A to the Code and entitled it 'Racist Crime.' This article provides that if an act is committed due to the perpetrator's hatred based on certain grounds, his/her sentence is increased. The new law adds colour, sexual orientation, gender identity and disability to the grounds of hatred existing in the previous article and enhances the sentences for hate crimes. Interestingly, the new provision of the Criminal Code is entitled 'Racist Crime' but does not, in fact, deal with racist crime only but with a variety of other crimes such as homophobic crimes. This discrepancy in the title of the article is reflective of the general limited definitional framework of the particular country. Moreover, although entitled racist crime, it essentially deals with aggravation and sentencing rather than a legal definition and conceptualisation of racist or hate crime.

1.1.4.4 Discrimination and Harassment

Law 474/1990, which ratified the ICERD, adopts the latter's definition of racial discrimination and, thereby, provides a definitional framework of this phenomenon for Greece. More particularly, Article 1(1) of the Law holds that:

> racial discrimination means any distinction, exclusion, restriction or preference based on race, colour, descent or national or ethnic origin which has the purpose or effect of nullifying or impairing the recognition, enjoyment or exercise on an equal footing, of human rights and fundamental freedoms in the political, economic, social, cultural or any other field of public life.[206]

---

206 Άρθρο 1(1) – υλετική διάκριση σημαίνει κάθε διάκριση, αποκλεισμό, περιορισμό ή προτίμηση με βάση τη φυλή, το χρώμα, την προέλευση ή την εθνική ή εθνοτική καταγωγή που έχει σκοπό

There is no definition of religious discrimination in any national legislation, case law or policy document.

Further, Law 3304/2005, which harmonises national law with the EU Equality Directives 2000/78/EC and 2000/43/EC, conceptualises discrimination with regard to the application of the principle of equal treatment and particularly direct and indirect discrimination in the manner set out in the directives with the former referring to less favourable treatment than another would have been given in a comparable situation[207] and the latter referring to an apparently neutral provision, criterion or practice that would put a person belonging to a particular group at a disadvantage compared to others.[208] The particular piece of legislation incorporates harassment or any other offensive conduct, which creates an intimidating, hostile, degrading, humiliating or offensive environment and which has the purpose or effect of, *inter alia*, creating a hostile, humiliating or aggressive environment, to fall within the definitional framework of discrimination.[209]

1.1.4.5 Public Order

This section will consider how public order is defined by national law. Greece's criminal order theoretically challenges the far-right through the anti-racist Law 927/1979, adding the element of public order as one of the requirements in finding an offence, such as incitement to racial hatred, as described below. Public order within the anti-racist law is a significant issue and, as such, analysis of the meaning of public order within the Greek legal order is necessary so as to facilitate a subsequent understanding of the applicable laws. Public order was briefly defined in the pre-trial report and the Prosecutor's recommendation. These documents note that public order is the 'serenity, tranquillity and peace and orderliness in the society of a state'[210] in which there exists 'a regulated

---

ή αποτέλεσμα την αναίρεση ή εξασθένιση της αναγνώρισης, απόλαυσης ή άσκησης, επί ίσοις όροις, των ανθρωπίνων δικαιωμάτων και των θεμελιωδών ελευθεριών στον πολιτικό, οικονομικό, κοινωνικό, πολιτισμικό ή άλλο τομέα της δημόσιας ζωής.

207 Article 3(1) and Article 7(1) of Law 3304/2005.
208 Article 3(b) and Article 7(1)(b) of Law 3304/2005.
209 Article 2 of Law 3304/2005.
210 Special Investigation Department: Athens Court of Appeal: Report to the President of the Greek Parliament regarding lifting the immunity of Golden Dawn members of parliament, Document Number 305 (19 February 2014) 8, Prosecutor's Recommendation to the Appeals Council regarding the Prosecution of Golden Dawn members and members

legal order, which threatens and imposes penalties against the offenders of legal rules, with the purposes of ensuring the exercise of individual, social or collective and state legal interests.'[211]

In light of the above, it is clear that the definitional framework of Greece in relation to terms relevant to the legislation that can be used to challenge the far-right is relatively lacking. This is because Greece does not contain many definitions within its legislation whilst the limited case law and policy on the matter prevent the existence of extensive interpretation of such terms. Either way some minimal extrapolation on terms facilitates an improved understanding of the legal framework.

---

of parliament (15 October 2014) 11: 'Δημόσια Τάξη είναι η κατάσταση γαλήνης, ηρεμίας, ειρήνης και ευταξίας στην κοινωνία ενός κράτους.'

211 Special Investigation Department: Athens Court of Appeal: Report to the President of the Greek Parliament regarding lifting the immunity of Golden Dawn members of parliament, Document Number 305 (19 February 2014) 8, 'η κατάσταση στην οποία προσβάλλονται με βλάβη η διακινδύνευση τα από αυτή επιλεγόμενα ως προστατευόμενα έννομα αγαθά του κοινωνικού συνόλου, ως αποτέλεσμα της ύπαρξης ρυθμιστικής έννομης τάξης, η οποία απειλεί και επιβάλλει κυρώσεις κατά των παραβατών κανόνων δικαίου με σκοπό να διατηρούνται αλώβητα τα ατομικά, κοινωνικά ή συλλογικά και κρατικά έννομα αγαθά.'

Chapter 2

The Treatment of Political Parties in the Greek Legal Order

2.1 Article 29: Legal Issues

Article 12 of the Greek constitution provides that 'Greeks shall have the right to form non-profit associations and unions, in compliance with the law, which, however, may never subject the exercise of this right to prior permission.'[1] Article 12 further holds, in part 2 thereof, that an association may only be dissolved by a court judgement and, in part 3 holds that this also applies to unions of persons which do not constitute an association. Although this article refers to non-profit associations and unions, there is no further extrapolation on what is meant by these terms apart from the reference to agricultural and urban co-operatives as a type of association and/or union. What becomes clear is that this article does not aim to cover political parties as an entity given that these are covered by a separate article dedicated exclusively to political parties, demonstrating the significance which the Greek legal order places on such entities.

Article 29 of the constitution provides that Greek citizens with the right to vote may establish and join political parties 'the organisation and activity of which must serve the free functioning of democratic government.'[2] Thus, the Greek constitution provides for the right to form and join political parties, without making any direct reference to limitation grounds of this right. While Article 29 of the Greek constitution provides that a party's organisation and activities shall serve the functioning of democracy, there are no processes or sanctions to ensure

---

1 Οι Έλληνες έχουν το δικαίωμα να συνιστούν ενώσεις και μη κερδοσκοπικά σωματεία, τηρώντας τους νόμους, που ποτέ όμως δεν μπορούν να εξαρτήσουν την άσκηση του δικαιώματος αυτού από προηγούμενη άδεια.

2 Έλληνες πολίτες που έχουν το εκλογικό δικαίωμα μπορούν ελεύθερα να ιδρύουν και να συμμετέχουν σε πολιτικά κόμματα, που η οργάνωση και η δράση τους οφείλει να εξυπηρετεί την ελεύθερη λειτουργία του δημοκρατικού πολιτεύματος.

DOI: 10.4324/9781003289302-2

compliance or punish violation of this tenet respectively. Specifically, no legal provisions were put forth concerning dissolution or prohibition of political parties in case this constitutional requirement is not met,[3] nor are there any essential registration requirements in place actually imposing any restrictions,[4] rendering this article a *lex imperfecta*. The situation, however, becomes complicated with Golden Dawn which, although a political party, was functioning simultaneously as a criminal organisation, raising issues pertaining to democratic order. Given the nature of Article 29, the only manner in which the state can challenge dangerous parties, including those of the far-right, is to tackle the particular actions of its members/leaders through the framework of criminal law, as was the case with Golden Dawn.

The broad constitutional protection provided to political parties is also reflected in the practicalities of the registration and functioning of parties. According to Article 29 of Law 3023/2002 on the Funding of Political Parties by the State, before engaging in political action, for a political party to be established, it must file a founding statement before the Supreme Court mentioning that its organisation and operation serves the democratic regime, in the spirit of Article 29 of the constitution. It must also notify the Supreme Court of the name, sign and seat of the political party and submit either its statutes or its founding statement signed by at least 200 citizens entitled to vote.[5] Therefore, a political party obtains legal personality by its establishment, for the fulfilment of its constitutional mission. However, in view of the aforementioned constitutional tradition, this is a purely formal procedure: the declarations of 'faith' to democracy are standardised and the Supreme Court has no mandate to ensure that a given party actually serves the free functioning of democracy in line with the constitution.[6] By simply pledging allegiance to the principles of Article 29 of the constitution on the necessity of a political party to serve a free functioning democracy, this does not necessarily mean that it sincerely aims to do so. Moreover, the Greek legal order has

---

3   Venice Commission (1999) (n 7) 19.
4   Ibid. 12.
5   Law 3023/2002 (OG A 146 20020625) 'Funding of Political Parties by the State, Income and Expenditure, Promotion, Advertising and Financial Auditing of Political Parties and Parliament Candidates.'
6   Kostas Mavrias, 'Constitutional law' (2003) (1st edn. P. N. Sakoulas, Athens) 394; Ioannis Drossos, 'The Legal Position of Political Parties in Greece' (1982) (1st edn. A. N. Sakoulas, Athens).

no tools which can be used for checking the sincerity of the required declaration.[7] As noted by the prosecutor of the Court of Cassation to the Council of Europe Commissioner of Human Rights, this procedure is not used to 'verify the lawfulness of the party concerned but acts in effect as a protocol book registering the applicant party.'[8] In fact, once there is an approval of the founding statement of the party, there seems to be no possibility for subsequently dismantling that party whilst there is no review process of the party's ongoing objectives and activities.[9] It must be highlighted that, even if there existed an obligation in Greek law for political parties to submit their statutes before the inception of their activities, this does not necessarily correlate with the ousting of, *inter alia*, far-right parties from existence. This is because camouflaging its real intentions and objectives within a constitution is not a complex task. Article 29(6) of Law 3023/2002 on the Financing of Political Parties by the State holds that, from the date of its inception, a political party gains a legal personality for the effectuation of its mission. Thus, a political party does not have to submit its statutes but can merely submit its founding statement that includes its adherence to serving the free functioning of a democratic state. So, a political party can have statutes which contain an array of fascist and/or racist statements and objectives but does not need to submit them to the state.

Another process which has given rise to interesting jurisprudence, is the one foreseen in the Presidential Decree 96/2007 on the Codification in a Single Text of the Provisions of the Legislation for the Election of Members of Parliament, according to which in order for a party to stand for a given election, it also has to file an application before the Supreme Court and the president of the parliament. This application only contains the name and the logo of the party. The only legal provisions which give the Supreme Court the margin to prohibit the participation of a party to an election relate to the name and sign thereof. More precisely, Article 37(5) of the above decree prohibits a party to use a name and sign related to the Greek flag, religious symbols, to kingship symbols and to symbols or emblems of the 1967 dictatorial regime, as well as

7   Dimitris Psaras, 'Golden Dawn before Justice' ('*Η Χρυσή Αυγή Μπροστά στη Δικαιοσύνη*') (1st edn. Rosa Luxemburg Foundation, Luxembourg 2014) 438.
8   Council of Europe Commissioner for Human Rights: Report on Greece, CommDH (2013) 6, 8.
9   European Commission against Racism and Intolerance: Report on Greece (24 February 2015) para. 26.

to use photographs of persons convicted for their participation in the dictatorship.[10] Examples of the prohibition of a name can be found in a 2012 case before the Court of Cassation regarding a political party entitled *Tyrannicides* (*Τυραννοκτόνοι*) that was prohibited from taking part in the May 2012 elections given that the court considered that this name demonstrated the intention to 'commit a criminal act'[11] and that this went against Article 29(1) of the constitution and Article 37(5) of the relevant presidential decree. However, all the party had to do was change its name to be able to take part in the elections. Thus, this approach demonstrates a certain level of superficiality in the constitutional approach to potentially dangerous political parties as it merely requested a change of name, making no inquest and assessment and taking no measures in relation to the party's objectives. In 2007, the Supreme Court had decided that the name '*New Fascism*' (*Νέος Φασισμός*), to which the candidate affiliated himself, was not allowed and that he would have to put forward his candidature without any affiliation to such a title as it goes against Article 37(5) of the above Presidential Decree in combination with Article 29(1) of the constitution.[12] Two issues can be concluded here. In the above cases, the judiciary was willing to take a broad approach to the meaning of Junta affiliated symbols and emblems as it considered the title '*New Fascism*' as well as '*Tyrannicides*' to fall within the framework of prohibited titles as provided for in Article 37(5). Secondly, banning a particular emblem or name does not necessarily correlate to ousting dangerous elements from the political scene of the country. In the cases examined, the court simply removed the problematic title attached to the applicant's candidature in one case and requested the political party to change its name in the other, with no meaningful impact on the functioning of democratic order.

In relation to the above, a comparison with the treatment of associations by the Civil Code of the Country is important. More particularly, Article 79, therein, provides that for purposes of registering an association, the founders or its management must submit an application to the competent court which includes its instrument of establishment, the names of the members of its administration and the association's statutes with the signatures of the members and the date. In fact, Article 80 of the Civil Code highlights the elements that need

---

10 Article 37(5) of the Presidential Decree 96/2007. See also PSARRAS D. (2015) (n 25) 14.
11 Case 4/2012: 'καταδεικνύει πρόθεση αξιόποινης πράξης.'
12 Case 4/2007.

to be incorporated in the constitution which include, amongst others, the association's objectives, membership and funding. As such, unlike a political party, an association must deposit its statutes which, as demonstrated in two cases which reached the ECtHR, are up for examination and scrutiny by the courts. In *Sidiropoulos and others v Greece*[13] and *L'affaire Maison de la Civilisation Macédonienne et Autres c. Grèce*,[14] Greece was in violation of Article 11 for refusing to register an association entitled the Home of Macedonian Civilisation (Στέγη Μακεδονικού Πολιτισμού). The second case arose following Greece's unwillingness to conform to the *Sidiropoulos* judgement. In both cases, the national judiciary had rejected the application for the association's formation on grounds pertaining to the dispute regarding the use of the name 'Macedonia.' As such, in relation to associations, the state and particularly the judiciary has the power to reject the formation of associations on grounds which it deems fit as these are not incorporated in the Civil Code. No equivalent restriction is available for political parties with the result that in Greece whilst parties such as Golden Dawn were allowed to register and subsequently enter the parliament, an association seeking to involve itself with a matter which is historically disputed (the use of the name 'Macedonia') has been prevented from registering as an association, regardless of an ECtHR ruling in its favour.

2.1.1 Article 2: History

Greek history and law have demonstrated a 'long-term hostility towards the phenomenon of the political party, culminating in the post-civil war prohibition of the KKE – Communist Party of Greece (KKE – Κομμουνιστικό Κόμμα Ελλάδας) and ended in 1975 with the fall of the dictatorship of 1967-1974 and the restoration of democracy.'[15] The Communist Party of Greece, the oldest party in modern Greek politics, was founded in 1918 and has 'drifted in and out of legality'[16] for about 30 years. In 1928, during Venizelos's rule, Law 4229/1929

---

13 *Sidiropoulos and Others v Greece*, App no. 57/197/841/1047 (ECHR 10 July 1998)

14 *L'affaire Maison de la Civilisation Macédonienne et Autres c. Grèce*, App. no. 1295/10 (ECHR 9 October 2015).

15 Kadir Aikout, 'Democracy under Threat and the judicial prohibition of Political Parties' (2021) *Curia.GR* available at: < https://curia.gr/dimokratia-ipo-apeili-kai-dikastiki -apagorefsi-politikon-kommaton/> [Accessed 28 November 2021].

16 Angela K. Bourne, 'Democratization and the Illegalization of Political Parties in Europe' (2012) 19 *Democratization* 6, 1077.

on Security Measures of Social Regime and the Protection of the
Freedom of Citizens rendered the Communist Party of Greece illegal.
Further, towards the end of the Civil War (1946–1949), the absolute
prohibition of the party came about through Law 509/1947 on the
Safety Measures of the State, the Social Regime and the Protection
of the Freedom of Citizens. Under this law, the Communist Party of
Greece was banned until 1974. Before this prohibition came about,
softer measures were enforced, such as the prohibition of pamphlets
of the Communist Party and other communist groups. For example, in 1947, the newspapers Ριζοσπάστης (*The Radical*) and Ελεύθερη
Ελλάδα (*Free Greece*) were prohibited.

On 21 April 1967, Greece experienced a military coup and subsequent Junta led by Colonel Papadopoulos. Political parties were banned,
political prisoners incarcerated and detained without trial and others sent
into exile. The resulting trauma 'redefined Greek politics.'[17] The Junta's
1968 constitution (Article 58(4) therein) created a puppet Constitutional
Court responsible for the 'continuous supervision' of political parties.
The court could dissolve such parties even if their actions were non-
violent. In brief, Greece has demonstrated a long-standing hostility to
political parties with the key characteristic being the long-term prohibition of the Communist Party of Greece.[18] Multiparty elections did not
take place during the Junta. Post-WWII Greece was 'indelibly marked
by the effort of a politically triumphant Greek right to institutionalize an
anticommunist state.'[19]

Greek constitutions until 1975 did not contain provisions on the
institution of political parties minus an indirect recognition of political parties in the constitutions of 1925 and 1927.[20] The constitution of 1952 contained no direct or indirect recognition of political
parties. Today, political parties are a 'condition sine qua non of the

---

17   Peteri Siani-Davies & Stefanos Katsikas, 'National Reconciliation after Civil War: The
     Case of Greece' (2009) 49 *Journal of Peace Research* 4, 565.
18   Nikolaos Mavrikas, '*The Legal Personality of Political Parties as an Element of their Activities,
     Theory and Practice of Administrative Law*' (Η Νομική Προσωπικότητα των Πολιτικών Κομμάτων ως
     στοιχείο Άσκησης της Δράσης τους.') (1st edn. Tefxos, Athens 2011).
19   Nikiforos Diamandouros, '1974: The Transition from the totalitarian to the democratic
     regime in Greece' (1983) 49 *Journal of Social Research*, 64.
20   Ν. Μαυρίκας, Η νομική προσωπικότητα των πολιτικών κομμάτων ως στοιχείο άσκησης της
     δράσης τους, Θεωρία και πράξη διοικητικού δικαίου, Τεύχος Ιουνίου 2011.

democratic state.'[21] The first constitution which recognised the political right of the establishment and participation in political parties is that of 1975, which demands such parties to cater for the functioning of a democratic system. The original draft of the constitution of 1975, stipulated that '(p)arties whose activity suggests an inclination to overthrow the free democratic system or to endanger the nation's territorial integrity may be outlawed under article 100 of the current Constitutional Court.' Nevertheless, this proposal was not retained[22] due to the harsh reaction of the opposition parties, whose concern was that such a provision would basically target the political parties of the left and the centre, and not the extreme right. It is important to underline that at the time, the centre and left political parties were sensitive to the issue, given that the Communist Party of Greece had been legalised only a few months earlier while the forces of the extreme right, including those in support of the recently overthrown military dictatorship, used to be active primarily through the so-called 'Deep State'[23] and paramilitary schemes,[24] rather than through political parties.

Following the fall of the dictatorship, Karamanlis returned from self-exile and became prime minister. Political stability was paramount so as to ensure bringing the colonels to justice without affecting the military, start democratisation in the country and negotiations in Cyprus (Turkish invasion followed the Greek *coup d'état*).[25] To achieve this stability, Karamanlis underlined the need for a 'genuine and progressive democracy' which has 'room for all Greeks.'[26] The ban on the Communist Party of Greece was lifted. As such, reconciliation in Greece emanated from the creation of a framework in which different narratives of the civil

21 Kadir Aikout, 'Democracy under Threat and the judicial prohibition of Political Parties' (2021) *Curia.GR* available at: < https://curia.gr/dimokratia-ipo-apeili-kai-dikastiki -apagorefsi-politikon-kommaton/> [Accessed 28 November 2021].

22 No Constitutional Court was finally formed. For this issue, ref. to Stefanos Mathias, 'Constitutional Justice in Greece', Science and Society, issue 11/2003 (in Greek).

23 Evi Gkotzaridis, 'Who Really Rules this Country? Collusion between State and Deep State in Post-Civil War Greece and the Murder of Independent MP Grigorios Lambrakis, 1958–1963' (2017) Diplomacy & Statecraft 28, no. 2, 646–673.

24 Spyridon Tsoutsoupis, 'The Far Right in Greece. Paramilitarism, Organized Crime and the Rise of 'Golden Dawn'' (2018) Südosteuropa 66.4, 503–531.

25 Peteri Siani-Davies & Stefanos Katsikas, 'National Reconciliation after Civil War: The Case of Greece' (2009) 49 *Journal of Peace Research* 4, 566.

26 The Times 26 July 1974.

war could be expressed. As such, reconciliation rested on 'a diversity of opinions.'[27]

The reluctance of the Greek legal order directly to incorporate immediate provisions to allow for the prohibition of political parties could potentially emanate from the country's experience with hostility held against certain political parties, particularly the Communist Party and the reconciliatory paradigm adopted by Karamanlis. In fact, during ECRI's most recent visit to Greece, many civil society organisations held that they would consider the banning of a political party 'with suspicion.'[28]

2.1.2 Article 29: Theoretical Issues

Prohibiting the functioning of a political party is not to be taken lightly. As noted by Bourne and Casal Bértoa, 'the challenges a party ban poses for core democratic principles make banning a party a grave act for democracy.'[29] As argued by Bourne, on the one hand a party ban is 'often the mark of authoritarianism' but on the other, may 'help protect democracies from their enemies and promote the rights of vulnerable citizens.'[30] To further understand the issue of party bans, this section will take a look at the theoretical backdrop of this issue. Militant democracy is a 'dominant point of departure in recent public and scholarly discussions on democratic self-defence.'[31] The doctrine of militant democracy (*wehrhafte Demokratie* or *streitbare Demokratie*) was developed by Loewenstein in 1937 who argued that 'democracy and democratic tolerance have been used for their own destruction.'[32] His position was that, 'until very recently, democratic fundamentalism and legalistic blindness were unwilling to realise that the mechanism of democracy is the

---

27   Peteri Siani-Davies & Stefanos Katsikas, 'National Reconciliation after Civil War: The Case of Greece' (2009) 49 *Journal of Peace Research* 4, 574.

28   European Commission against Racism and Intolerance: Report on Greece (24 February 2015) para. 26.

29   Angela Bourne & Fernando Casal Bértoa, 'Mapping Militant Democracy: Variation in Party Ban Practices in European Democracies (1945–2015)' (2017) 13 *European Constitutional Law Review*, 223.

30   Ibid.

31   Capoccia 2013, Kirshner 2014, Muller 2012, Sajo 2004 as discussed in Anthoula Malkopoulou & Ludvig Norman, 'Three Models of Democratic Self-Defence: Militant Democracy and its Alternatives' (2018) 66 *Political Studies* 22, 442.

32   Karl Loewenstein, 'Militant Democracy and Fundamental Rights I' (1937) 31 *The American Political Science Review* 3, 423.

Trojan horse by which the enemy enters the city.'[33] As a result, he recommended that 'constitutions … have to be stiffened and hardened' and
that 'every possible effort must be made to rescue [democracy], even at
risk and cost of violating fundamental principles.'[34] Relevant to this doctrine are Popper's thoughts on an open society in which he spoke of the
'paradox of tolerance,'[35] highlighting that 'unlimited tolerance must lead
to the disappearance of tolerance.'[36]

Following Nazi atrocities, the German Basic Law became the first
European constitution to endorse militant democracy, with most post-
WWII constitutions following its example[37] (to varying levels). Militant
democracy has been discussed and described by several scholars over
time.[38] In fact, in recent years, the doctrine has 'gained renewed sali-
ence in light of political developments across Europe and the US where
extremist political movements are on the rise.'[39] Harvey states that it is
a system which is 'capable of defending the constitution against anti-
democratic actors who use the democratic process in order to subvert
it.'[40] Pfersmann argues that it is a 'political and legal structure aimed at
preserving democracy against those who want to overturn it from within
or those who openly want to destroy it from outside by utilizing democratic institutions as well as support within the population.'[41]

Pfersmann argues that 'democracies are always more or less militant.'[42]
Posner underlines that any liberal constitution should take measures in

---

33   Ibid. 424.
34   Ibid. 432.
35   As explained in Karl Popper 'The Open Society and Its Enemies' (published in two vol-
umes: *The Spell of Plato and The High Tide of Prophecy: Hegel, Marx, and the Aftermath*) (1st
edn. Routledge, London 1945) 546.
36   Ibid.
37   Paul Harvey, 'Militant Democracy and the European Convention on Human Rights'
(2004) 29 *European Law Review* 3, 408.
38   See, for example, Patrick Macklem, 'Militant Democracy, Legal Pluralism, and the Paradox
of Self-determination' (2005) 4 *International Journal of Constitutional Law* 3, Paul Harvey,
'Militant Democracy and the European Convention on Human Rights' (2004) 29 *European
Law Review* 3.
39   Anthoula Malkopoulou & Ludvig Norman, 'Three Models of Democratic Self-Defence:
Militant Democracy and its Alternatives' (2018) 66 *Political Studies* 22, 442.
40   Paul Harvey, 'Militant Democracy and the European Convention on Human Rights'
(2004) 29 *European Law Review* 3, 408.
41   Otto Pfersmann, 'Shaping Militant Democracy: Legal Limits to Democratic Stability' in
Andras Sajó (ed), 'Militant Democracy' (1st edn. Eleven International Publishing, Utrecht
2004) 47.
42   Ibid. 53.

self-defence.[43] Sajó highlights that the state's most natural characteristic is self-defence.[44] Nevertheless, Macklem argues that 'the legality of militant democracy ... is far from clear.'[45] Sajó warns of the doctrine's 'potentially expansive reach'[46] since 'a militant democracy can easily become an illiberal democracy, more concerned with its own stability than with political developments.'[47] Accetti and Zuckerman hold that there exists the 'irreducible element of arbitrariness in whichever way the decision is taken as to what constitutes an enemy of democracy.'[48]

Turning to the book's context, the question posed is whether Greece is a militant democracy. As argued by Malkopoulou, this depends on how broadly we define the term.[49] If the doctrine is conceptualised as constitutional or legal provisions allowing for the banning of political parties, then no, Greece is not a militant democracy. However, restrictions to human rights and fundamental freedoms such as that of expression are contained in pieces of legislation such as the anti-racist law.

Banning a political party remains a 'dilemma for democracies.'[50] This is particularly so for Greece due to its traumatic history during the Junta but also the civil war. The restitution of this trauma has been translated into the country's legal order offering 'ample protection to political parties'[51] and a general 'aversion towards party bans.'[52] To provide a theoretical backdrop to Greece's approach, one must turn to Kelsen's procedural model which is the country's chosen democratic model. Kelsen was

43   Richard A. Posner, 'Not a Suicide Pact: The Constitution in a Time of National Emergency' (1st edn. Oxford University Press, Oxford 2006).

44   András Sajó, 'Militant Democracy and Transition towards Democracy' in Andras Sajó (ed), 'Militant Democracy' (1st edn. Eleven International Publishing, Utrecht 2004) 213.

45   Patrick Macklem, 'Militant Democracy, Legal Pluralism, and the Paradox of Self-determination' (2005) 4 International Journal of Constitutional Law 3, 488.

46   András Sajó, 'Militant Democracy and Emotional Politics' (2012) 19 Constellations 4, 565: https://onlinelibrary.wiley.com/doi/pdf/10.1111/cons.12011 [Accessed 12 July 2021].

47   John E. Finn, 'Constitutions in Crisis: Political Violence and the Rule of Law' (1st edn. Oxford University Press, Oxford 1991) 217.

48   Carlo Invernizzi Accetti1 & Ian Zuckerman, 'What's Wrong with Militant Democracy?' (2017) 65 Political Studies IS, 183.

49   Anthoula Malkopoulou, 'Greece: A Procedural Defense of Democracy against the Golden Dawn' (2021) 17 European Constitutional Law Review 181.

50   Angela K. Bourne, 'Democratization and the Illegalization of Political Parties in Europe' (2012) 19 Democratization 6, 1065.

51   Anthoula Malkopoulou, 'Greece: A Procedural Defense of Democracy against the Golden Dawn' (2021) 17 European Constitutional Law Review 182.

52   Ibid.

Loewenstein's 'chief challenger in the interwar years and onwards'[53] who argued that when a democracy attempts to safeguard itself from anti-democratic entities, it is no longer a democracy.[54] Kelsen's approach of a procedural model 'rejects the constitutionalisation of repressive and exclusionary measures and stresses openness and pluralism as democracy's unconditional principles.'[55] At the core of Kelsen's model lies the rejection of substantive moral values and support of 'clearly established, value-neutral, legal procedures that promote negative freedom.'[56] As such, the prohibition of political parties is deemed undemocratic and illiberal.

Whilst the procedural model prohibits the banning of political parties, it does allow for the introduction of, for example, anti-racist laws since such laws do not prohibit the underlying ideology as such but, instead, exist so as to punish the use of subsequent harm on other individuals. Such laws are permissible insofar as they are narrow enough to be directly linked to the prevention of imminent physical harm.[57]

2.1.3 Article 29 and ECtHR Case Law

To dissect further the legal aspects of Article 29 (and the non-inclusion of a party ban clause), this section turns to the approach of the ECtHR in relation to the prohibition of political parties.

2.1.3(i) Article 11 ECHR

Article 11 of the ECHR provides for the qualified right to the freedom of assembly and association. It stipulates that:

1. Everyone has the right to freedom of peaceful assembly and to freedom of association with others, including the right to form and to join trade unions for the protection of his interests.

---

53 Anthoula Malkopoulou & Ludvig Norman, 'Three Models of Democratic Self-Defence: Militant Democracy and its Alternatives' (2018) 66 *Political Studies* 22, 448.

54 Paul Cliteur & Bastiaan Rijpkema, 'The Foundations of Militant Democracy' in Afshin Ellian & Gelijn Molier (ed), 'The State of Exception and Militant Democracy in a Time of Terror' (1st edn. Republic of Letters Publishing, Dordrecht 2012) 243.

55 Anthoula Malkopoulou & Ludvig Norman, 'Three Models of Democratic Self-Defence: Militant Democracy and its Alternatives' (2018) 66 *Political Studies* 22, 443.

56 Anthoula Malkopoulou, 'Greece: A Procedural Defense of Democracy against the Golden Dawn' (2021) 17 *European Constitutional Law Review* 187.

57 Ibid. 195.

2. No restrictions shall be placed on the exercise of these rights other than such as are prescribed by law and are necessary in a democratic society in the interests of national security or public safety, for the prevention of disorder or crime, for the protection of health or morals or for the protection of the rights and freedoms of others. This Article shall not prevent the imposition of lawful restrictions on the exercise of these rights by members of the armed forces, of the police or of the administration of the State.

In *United Communist Party of Turkey and Others v Turkey* (1998), the court underlined the essential role political parties play in ensuring pluralism and the proper functioning of democracy.[58] As such, in the framework of party bans, Article 11 limitation grounds must be 'construed strictly; only convincing and compelling reasons can justify restrictions on such parties' freedom of association.'[59] *Refah Partisi v Turkey* dealt with the dissolution of an Islamic political party and the suspension of the political rights of the other applicants who were leaders of the party at that time. There, the ECtHR underlined that 'only convincing and compelling reasons can justify restrictions on such parties' freedom of association.'[60] In relation to the pursuit of a legitimate aim, in *Refah Partisi*, the court found that, in light of the importance of secularism in Turkey, the interference pursued the legitimate aim of protecting national security and public safety, prevention of disorder or crime and protection of the rights and freedoms of others.[61] Thus, the analysis of the legitimate aim occurred against the backdrop of secularism, with the court taking into account an appraisal of the situation in the state under consideration and, specifically, the 'general interest in preserving the principle of secularism in that context in the country'[62] as well as its own previous statements of secularism being a fundamental principle in line with the rule of law, human rights and democracy.[63] When assessing restrictions, 'the right of association is accorded particular protection in the maintenance of pluralist opinion

---

58   *United Communist Party of Turkey and Others v Turkey* (1998), Para 43
59   Ibid. para. 46.
60   *Refah Partisi (the Welfare Party) and Others v Turkey*, Application nos. 41340/98, 41342/98 and 41344/98 (ECHR 13 February 2003) para. 100
61   *Refah Partisi (the Welfare Party) and Others v Turkey*, Application nos. 41340/98, 41342/98 and 41344/98 (ECHR 13 February 2003) para. 67
62   Ibid. para. 105.
63   Ibid. para. 93.

and democracy.'[64] In determining whether the restriction is necessary in a democratic society, the court must ascertain whether there is a pressing social need for the restriction. To do so, it considers three factors, namely whether a risk to democracy is sufficiently imminent, whether the acts and speeches of the leaders and members of the political party were imputable to the party as a whole and whether the acts and speeches imputable to the political party promoted a societal model incompatible with the concept of a democratic society.[65] Further, the court looks at the contextual and, sometimes, historical setting in which a particular dissolution occurs. For example, in *Refah Partisi*, the court considered the general interest in preserving secularism in Turkey.[66] Context was also significant in other Article 11 cases, such as *Herri Batasuna and Batasuna v Spain*, where the court underlined that, in view of the Spanish experience with terrorist attacks, a link with Euskadi Ta Askatasuna (ETA) and the applicant parties could objectively result in a threat to democracy.[67] Further, the prohibition must be proportional to the legitimate aim pursued. In *Refah Partisi*, the court noted 'that the nature and severity of the interference are ... factors to be taken into account when assessing its proportionality.'[68] In *Herri Batasuna and Batasuna v Spain*, the court held that, in order to determine whether an interference was proportionate to the legitimate aim pursued, it must consider it in light of the case as a whole.[69] In *Refah Partisi*, the court noted that, after the party's dissolution, only five of its MPs temporarily forfeited their parliamentary office and their role as leaders of a political party. The remaining 152 MPs continued to sit in parliament.

---

64 Mustafa Koçak & Esin Örücü, 'Dissolution of political parties in the Name of Democracy: Cases from Turkey and the European Court of Human Rights' (2003) 9 *European Public Law* 3, 419.

65 *Refah Partisi (the Welfare Party) and Others v Turkey*, Application nos. 41340/98, 41342/98 and 41344/98 (ECHR 13 February 2003) para. 104 (this test was also implemented in *Vona v Hungary*).

66 Ibid. para. 105.

67 *Herri Batasuna and Batasuna v Spain*, Application nos. 25803/04 and 25817/04 (ECHR 6 November 2009) para. 89

68 Refah Partisi (the Welfare Party) and Others v Turkey, Application nos. 41340/98, 41342/98 and 41344/98 (ECHR 13 February 2003) para. 133

69 Herri Batasuna and Batasuna v Spain, Application nos. 25803/04 and 25817/04 (ECHR 6 November 2009) para. 75.

2.1.3(ii) The Questions of Democracy and Violence

The ECtHR has highlighted the interrelationship between the functioning of political parties and the preservation of democracy. In *Socialist
Party and Others v Turkey*, the ECtHR noted that 'political parties are a
form of association, and that, in view of the importance of democracy in
the Convention system, there can be no doubt that political parties come
within the scope of Article 11.'[70] In *United Communist Party of Turkey
and Others v Turkey*, the court stated that 'in view of the role played by
political parties, any measure taken against them affected both freedom
of association and, consequently, democracy in the State concerned.'[71] In
this case, it also emphasised the particular importance of political parties
(when compared with other forms of associations) given that 'by the proposal for an overall societal model which they put before the electorate
and by their capacity to implement those proposals once they come to
power, political parties differ from other organisations which intervene
in the political arena.'[72] In *Dicle (on behalf of the Democratic Party (DEP))
v Turkey*, the court stated that, to ensure a functional democracy, political bodies should be able to make public proposals, even if they are in
conflict with mainstream governmental policy or prevailing public opinion.[73] The court emphasised the need to protect political parties vigor-
ously 'in view of their essential role in ensuring pluralism and the proper
functioning of democracy.'[74] In fact, it has repeatedly underlined that the
dissolution of a political party and the restriction of party members from
carrying out their activities for a particular time period are measures to
be resorted to only in the most serious of cases.[75]

However, the court notes that a political party can work towards its
aim only if 'the means used to that end must be legal and democratic ...
[and] the change proposed must itself be compatible with fundamental

---

70   *Socialist Party and Others v Turkey*, Application no. 21237/83 (ECHR 25 May 1998)

71   *United Communist Party of Turkey and Others*, Application no. 19392/92 (ECHR 30 January
     1998) para. 31.

72   *Refah Partisi (the Welfare Party) and Others v Turkey*, Application nos. 41340/98, 41342/98
     and 41344/98 (ECHR 13 February 2003) para. 87.

73   *Dicle (on behalf of the Democratic Party DEP) v Turkey*, Application no. 25141/94 (10 January
     2012) para. 53.

74   *Refah Partisi (the Welfare Party) and Others v Turkey*, Application nos. 41340/98, 41342/98
     and 41344/98 (ECHR 13 February 2003) para. 88.

75   See *United Communist Party of Turkey and Others*, *Socialist Party and Others*, cited earlier, and
     Freedom and Democracy Party (ÖZDEP) v Turkey.

democratic principles.'[76] As noted in cases such as *Batasuna* and *Socialist Party*, the following points need to be considered (i) whether there was plausible evidence that the risk to democracy, supposing it had been proved to exist, was sufficiently and reasonably imminent, and (ii) whether the acts and speeches imputable to the political party formed a whole which gave a clear picture of a model of society conceived and advocated by the party which was incompatible with the concept of a 'democratic society.' In *Refah Partisi*, the court considered that the 'constitution and programme of a political party cannot be taken into account as the sole criterion for determining its objectives and intentions.'[77] As a result, the court noted that:

> the content of the programme must be compared with the actions of the party's leaders and the positions they defend. Taken together, these acts and stances may be relevant in proceedings for the dissolution of a political party, provided that as a whole they disclose its aims and intentions.[78]

Further, the court held that the dissolution of a political party with an anti-democratic mandate is 'also consistent with Contracting Parties' positive obligations under Article 1 of the Convention to secure the rights and freedoms of persons within their jurisdiction.'[79] It should also be necessary in a democratic society.

In relation to violence, in *Herri Batasuna and Batasuna*, the court highlighted that

> a political party whose leaders incite to violence or put forward a policy which fails to respect democracy, or which is aimed at the destruction of democracy and the flouting of the rights and freedoms recognised in a democracy cannot lay claim to the Convention's protection against penalties imposed on those grounds.[80]

---

76   *Refah Partisi (the Welfare Party) and Others v Turkey*, Application nos. 41340/98, 41342/98 and 41344/98 (ECHR 13 February 2003) para. 98.

77   *Refah Partisi (the Welfare Party) and Others v Turkey*, Application nos. 41340/98, 41342/98 and 41344/98 (ECHR 13 February 2003) para. 101.

78   Ibid.

79   Ibid. para. 103.

80   *Herri Batasuna and Batasuna v Spain*, Application nos. 25803/04 and 25817/04 (ECHR 6 November 2009) para. 49.

In *Refah Partisi*, the court considered that the members of the party in question mentioned the possibility of resorting to force to overcome the obstacles that *Refah Partisi* was facing in the political arena.[81] The court recognised that, while its leaders did not, in government documents, call for the use of force and violence as a political weapon, 'they did not take prompt practical steps to distance themselves from those members of [*Refah*] who had publicly referred with approval to the possibility of using force against politicians who opposed them.'[82]

2.1.3(iii) The Question of Timing

The intricately complex question of timing in the realm of dissolution of associations must be considered with due care to avoid unsubstantiated actions which constitute a breach of Article 11, on the one hand, whilst avoiding harmful consequences of destructive associations on the other. In *Refah Partisi v Turkey*, the court held that a state may reasonably prevent the execution of a policy which is against the letter and spirit of the Convention. The court also underlined that:

> A State cannot be required to wait, before intervening, until a political party has seized power and begun to take concrete steps to implement a policy incompatible with the standards of the Convention and democracy, even though the danger of that policy for democracy is sufficiently established and imminent.[83]

2.1.3(iv) Concluding Comments

Enforcing Article 11 limitation grounds to the prohibition of a political party has to be conducted stringently and with care. It is clear that political parties which aim for the destruction of democracy and/or which endorse and or use violence to achieve their objectives cannot enjoy Convention protection against penalties imposed on those grounds. Therefore, 'only convincing and compelling reasons can justify restrictions on such parties' freedom of association.[84] Greece does not follow

---

81   *Refah Partisi (the Welfare Party) and Others v Turkey*, Application nos. 41340/98, 41342/98 and 41344/98 (ECHR 13 February 2003) para. 130.
82   Ibid. para. 131.
83   Ibid. para. 102.
84   Ibid. para. 100.

suit on the position of the ECtHR as it does not constitutionally allow for the banning of a political party.

2.1.4 Impact of Article 29 on Golden Dawn

It is thus clear that in Greece there is no constitutional allowance for banning political parties. This issue, however, became rather complicated in 2013, with the unprecedented prosecution of Golden Dawn, a registered political party and a criminal organisation.[85] A few weeks after the June 2012 elections, the Council of Europe Commissioner of Human Rights held that, although Greek legislation does not clearly provide for the prohibition of political parties, Article 29(1) refers to the requirement that such parties must serve the free function of democratic government. He then posed a rhetorical question as to whether Golden Dawn serves the free functioning of democratic government.[86] The Commissioner argued that the qualification found in Article 29 (namely that a political party must serve the free functioning of democratic government) could be 'interpreted according to the principle of *effet utile* in a way that would give a practical meaning to the above constitutional meanings.'[87] More particularly, the Commissioner recommended the adoption of relevant legislation or development of jurisprudence which would give effect to the aforementioned qualification and 'restrict or prohibit, if necessary, a party for which ample evidence demonstrates that it does not serve the free functioning of democratic governance.'[88] In making this recommendation, the Commissioner reiterated that such measures would be in conformity with Greece's obligations under Article 4 of the ICERD and Article 11 and Article 17 of the ECHR.[89] Further, in its 2009 Concluding Observations to Greece, the UN's Committee on the Elimination of all Forms of Racial Discrimination (CERD) recommended that the state party 'concretely ban neo-nazi groups from its territory.'[90] When con-

---

85   Dimitris Christopoulos., 'The Golden Dawn trial: A Major Event for Democracy in Greece and Beyond'. (2018) OpenDemocracy.

86   Dimitris Psaras, '*The Black Bible of Golden Dawn: The Documented History of a Nazi Group*' ('*Η Μαύρη Βίβλος της Χρυσής Αυγής, Ντοκουμέντα από την Ιστορία και τη Δράση μιας Ναζιστικής Ομάδας*) (1st edn. Polis 2012) 445.

87   Council of Europe Commissioner for Human Rights – Report on Greece, CommDH(2013) 6, 8.

88   Ibid.

89   Ibid. 9.

90   ICERD Concluding Observations – Greece, CERD/C/GRC/CO/19 (2009) 11.

fronted with the issue of Golden Dawn, the state habitually reiterated the position that the Greek constitutional order does not provide for the prohibition of political parties. However, as noted in the pre-trial report, the requirement of Article 29 that political parties serve the free functioning of a democratic state means that an organisation such as Golden Dawn is not protected under Article 29.[91] This is because, under the guise of a political party, Golden Dawn demonstrated its real objectives with the use of, amongst other things, physical and armed violence and threats against life. The report further noted that the use of Article 29 for such purposes constitutes a violation of Article 25(3) of the constitution on the non-abuse of rights.[92] In light of this position, the pre-trial report found that it was legally possible to find members and leaders of a criminal organisation which posed as a political party guilty of offences under Article 187 of the Criminal Code.

One of the few times the issue of banning Golden Dawn reached the parliament was in 1998. The Minister of Justice held that Golden Dawn is 'clear fascism. And as fascism it is a murderous act, a murderous ideology against the state.'[93] However, he continued to note that care must be taken so that others do not say that 'in Greece ideas are persecuted.'[94] Although an examination and discussion of the situation was instructed, this never took place. So, even in 1998, the state recognised the dangers posed by this party but never took constructive steps to move against it. Steps have also been taken by civil society in the realm of the party's prohibition. Namely, in 2011, the Greek Helsinki Monitor filed a court claim requesting the District Attorney to commence procedures for banning Golden Dawn given that it violates Article 37.5 of Presidential Decree 96/2007 in combination with Article 29(1) of the constitution. In the application, reference was made to the Nazi salutes of party members and references and photographs of the Nazi activity of Golden Dawn, but to no avail. ECRI noted that 'timely action'[95]

---

91   Special Investigation Department: Athens Court of Appeal: Report to the President of the Greek Parliament regarding lifting the immunity of Golden Dawn members of parliament, Document Number 305. 19 February 2014, 20.

92   Ibid. 11.

93   Greek Parliament official minutes – Deliberation 18/2/1998: 'Είναι καθαρός φασισμός. Και ως φασισμός είναι δολοφονική πράξη, δολοφονική ιδεολογία εναντίον του πολιτεύματος.'

94   Greek Parliament official minutes – Deliberation 18/2/1998: 'πρέπει να εξετάσουμε το θέμα. Μην περιπέσουμε σε καμία άκρη και λένε ότι στην Ελλάδα διώκονται οι ιδέες.'

95   European Commission against Racism and Intolerance: Report on Greece (24 February 2015) para. 26.

should have been taken against such parties so as to 'avoid an escalation of criminal activities.'[96]

The above approach adopted by the Greek state towards the prohibition of political parties resulted in a considerable weakness as it was unable to tackle effectively and dismantle, amongst others, far-right elements which organise themselves in the form of a political party. It is also reasonable to assume that the sacred constitutional status of political parties affected the delayed reaction of the state within the ambit of the Criminal Code. The viewpoint adopted almost unequivocally by the Greek political system was that it was impossible to ban the party in its entirety given that the Greek constitutional order does not provide for the prohibition of political parties.[97] As a result of this certainty, each time a member of Golden Dawn was involved in the perpetration of a violent activity, the competent authorities avoided the investigation of the perpetrator's link to Golden Dawn[98] and, subsequently, the ramifications of this interrelationship on the status of Golden Dawn as a political party. Moreover, on some occasions, relevant incidents carried out by Golden Dawn reached the parliament with the Ministry of Justice habitually condemning Nazism whilst systematically noting that an ideology cannot be persecuted, only actions.[99] The direct consequences of the state's stance was that, in the name of an absolute freedom to establish and participate in political parties, Golden Dawn was not dismantled, which contributed to its violent actions remaining unfettered.

2.1.5 The Doctrine of Parliamentary Immunity and Public Funding

The doctrine of parliamentary immunity is fundamental to the functioning of a democracy and the regulation of powers of the different branches of the state. The legislature is one of the most significant branches of a state because as well as its legislative actions 'it also monitors the executive body and holds it accountable for the execution of its duties.'[100] As such, MPs are granted legal protections to facilitate their activities. Agreeing

---

96 Ibid.
97 Dimitris Psaras, 'Golden Dawn before Justice' ('Η Χρυσή Αυγή Μπροστά στη Δικαιοσύνη') (1st edn. Rosa Luxemburg Foundation, Berlin 2014) 10
98 Ibid.
99 Ibid
100 Amal Yusuf Alrfua, Ahmad Hasan Abu Sabah & Ayman Yousef Mutlaq Alrfoua, 'Parliamentary Immunity in International Legislation' (2018) 14 Asian Social Science 6, 71.

on a definition of parliamentary immunity is not an easy task, particularly given that this doctrine takes different forms, even within Europe. A broad-ranging understanding of parliamentary immunity would consider the doctrine as any prohibition of legal action, investigation and enforcement of the law (civil or criminal) against parliamentarians. Taking the European framework, much of the content adopts the model initially embraced by France whereby the inviolability of MPs accompanies the non-accountability. Thus, MPs are not held accountable for their parliamentary behaviour and, in theory, cannot be incarcerated without parliament lifting their immunity. Scholars recognise that parliamentary immunity is 'indispensable to the operation of democracy.'[101] On the other hand, some are concerned with the possibilities that parliamentary immunity gives parliamentarians licence to 'pursue their own personal and political interests, over and above that which is made possible simply by their position of influence,'[102] something which by default goes against the core of the doctrine and democracy itself.

The Greek legal system provides for enhanced protection for the activities of MPs, limiting, to the extent possible, any censorship or restriction from the state. As with Article 29 of the constitution, this doctrine and the extent of its protection in the Greek legal order can be linked back to the prohibitionism and censorship which marked the periods of the civil war and the colonels' regime. Within the spirit of reconciliation and pursuit of pluralism, Greece opted for an open and liberal democracy with little interference in political rights. Nevertheless, parliamentary immunity in Greece has certain restrictions (as opposed to the functioning of political parties). The principle of parliamentary immunity is protected by Article 62 of the constitution which holds that 'during the parliamentary term the MPs shall not be prosecuted, arrested, imprisoned or otherwise confined without prior leave granted by parliament.'[103] However, this article provides that 'no leave is required when MPs are caught in the act of committing a felony.' On the last point regarding felonies, in 2012 and following the increase in violence perpetrated against groups

---

101 Observations of the Dutch Government, annexed to the judgement in *A v The United Kingdom*, App. No 35373/97 (ECHR 17 December 2002).

102 Simon Wigley, 'Parliamentary Immunity: Defending Democracy or Defending Corruption?' (2003) 2 *Journal of Political Philosophy* 11, 23.

103 Όσο διαρκεί η βουλευτική περίοδος ο βουλευτής δεν διώκεται ούτε συλλαμβάνεται ούτε φυλακίζεται ούτε με άλλο τρόπο περιορίζεται χωρίς άδεια του Σώματος. Επίσης δεν διώκεται για πολιτικά εγκλήματα βουλευτής της Βουλής που διαλύθηκε, από τη διάλυσή της και έως την ανακήρυξη των βουλευτών της νέας Βουλής.

such as migrants and arbitrary identification checks by groups of citizens which also included MPs, a new circular was prepared regarding the issue of impunity. This circular allows for the arrest of MPs if they commit a felony even if parliamentary immunity has not been lifted.[104] Further, following Fyssas's murder, the parliament voted to lift this immunity so that they could be tried.

In addition to parliamentary immunity, public funding of political parties is also a tool facilitating their democratic mandate. Following the arrests of the Golden Dawn leadership in 2013, the Greek parliament amended Law 3023/2002 and, in this way, decided that public funding may be ceased if a party's leader or head of the parliamentary group or one fifth of its MPs are charged with involvement in a criminal or terrorist organisation. If the defendants had been found not guilty then the suspended funds would have been returned to the party.

2.1.6 Concluding Comments: Freedom of Association and Political Parties in Greece

It appears to be a relatively easy task to register a political party in Greece, so long as you have no emblems or symbols related to the Junta, your registration is supported by 200 signatures and you pledge allegiance to the free functioning of a democratic state. In addition to this, the state's ongoing approach has been that the Greek legal order does not allow for the prohibition of political parties. Thus, it is not only easy to register as a political party and hide your true intentions but it is also easy to continue functioning as one without the fear of prohibition unless, as with the case of Golden Dawn, your activities move into the realm of a criminal organisation. In fact, the only constructive measure the state may take against a party is the suspension of public funding in cases of serious criminal offences committed by its members and/or leadership and the prosecution of its MPs. According to the situation, as described above, this can take place with or without lifting their immunity, thereby allowing a broad intervention of the state when it comes to individual criminal responsibility. As such, unless the activities or rhetoric of a political party meet the high thresholds of a criminal organisation, it can seemingly act and speak freely in Greece, notwithstanding existing anti-racist

104 Athanasios Theodoridis, 'Report on Measures to Combat Discrimination – Directives 2000/43/EC and 2000/78/EC – Country Report 2013 – State of affairs up to 1 January 2014) European Network of Legal Experts in the Non-discrimination field' 134.

legislation that prohibits, *inter alia*, organisations that incite racial or religious hatred or violence. Given the sanctity of political parties in the Greek legal order such a law could not reasonably be expected to extend to them. In understanding Greece's position on the question, namely the banning of a political party, one must take into account the history and post-Junta reconciliatory model discussed above, the resulting procedural rather than militant approach to democratic functioning and the fact that Article 29 is a *lex imperfecta* since it does set out a condition but does not accompany that with a process of sanction.

Chapter 3

Human Rights Law

3.1 Human Rights: Conceptual Backdrop

Article 2(1) of the Greek constitution holds that 'respect and protection of the value of the human being constitute the primary obligations of the state.'[1] Personal freedom is established by Article 5(1), but this is not absolute given that this is permissible 'insofar as they do not infringe the rights of others or violate the constitution or morals.'[2] The constitution contains a non-destruction clause in the form of Article 25(3) which holds that 'the abusive exercise of rights is not permitted.'[3] As such, militant democracy and the need to protect society and others from destructive forces emanating from abusive use of rights and freedoms is codified on a national level in the country's constitution. The constitution provides for the freedom of expression, freedom of assembly and freedom of association, which are all tools habitually used and abused by the far-right with Greece constituting a primordial example of such abuse with Golden Dawn having acted with a state of impunity for several years, advancing itself, its rhetoric and acts and calling upon the freedoms above as the means to do so. In relation to the freedom of association, it must be underlined that political parties hold a particularly significant place in the Greek Legal Order and a certain overprotection thereof may be deemed to exist. The almost absolutist approach adopted by the

---

1 'Ο σεβασμός και η προστασία της αξίας του ανθρώπου αποτελούν την πρωταρχική υποχρέωση της Πολιτείας.'
2 'Ο καθένας έχει δικαίωμα να αναπτύσσει ελεύθερα την προσωπικότητά του και να συμμετέχει στην κοινωνική, οικονομική και πολιτική ζωή της Χώρας, εφόσον δεν προσβάλλει τα δικαιώματα των άλλων και δεν παραβιάζει το Σύνταγμα ή τα χρηστά ήθη.'
3 'Η καταχρηστική άσκηση δικαιώματος δεν επιτρέπεται.'

DOI: 10.4324/9781003289302-3

non-prohibition of political parties has had a significant effect on the handling of Golden Dawn.

3.1.1 Freedom of Expression

Freedom of expression is provided for in Article 14 of the constitution which is entitled 'Freedom of the Press.' Part (1) of this article holds that 'every person may express and propagate his thoughts orally, in writing and through the press in compliance with the laws of the state.'[4] Parts (2)–(9) of the article focus solely on the press. Thus, the constitution essentially provides for free expression with the sole restriction being that such expression must comply with national laws. Rather than separating freedom of opinion and expression, the constitution refers to the freedom of expression and the freedom to propagate such expression. However, it could hardly be argued that the constitution does not provide for opinion, it is simply the case that it incorporates free expression as if it were opinion, separating the right to propagate such expression. Further, Article 16(1) of the constitution, on education, art and sciences, holds that 'art and science, research and teaching shall be free and their development and promotion shall be an obligation of the state. Academic freedom and freedom of teaching shall not exempt anyone from his duty of allegiance to the constitution.'[5] This provision is relevant to expression which is propagated through, for example, artistic means, but also in relation to academic freedom and the issues that have arisen in the framework of academia under the amended anti-racist law and the handling of genocides and other international crimes.[6] It is noteworthy that the freedom of expression constituted the basic reasoning put forth by those opposed to the 2014 amendments to the anti-racist law.[7]

In addition to free expression having been cited several times as a reason for rejecting the 2014 amendments to the anti-racist law, this freedom has heavily marked the Supreme Court's discussion of one of the few cases which occurred within the framework of the anti-racist

---

4   'Καθένας μπορεί να εκφράζει και να διαδίδει προφορικά, γραπτά και δια του τύπου τους στοχασμούς του τηρώντας τους νόμους του Κράτους.'

5   '1. Η τέχνη και η επιστήμη, η έρευνα και η διδασκαλία είναι ελεύθερες η ανάπτυξη και η προαγωγή τους αποτελεί υποχρέωση του Κράτους. Η ακαδημαϊκή ελευθερία και η ελευθερία της διδασκαλίας δεν απαλλάσσουν από το καθήκον της υπακοής στο Σύνταγμα.'

6   For example, Heinz Richter's case.

7   Explanatory Report for amendments to Law 927/1979.

law 927/1979, namely that against Constantinos Plevris[8] for the publishing of his book *Jews – The Whole Truth* (Εβραίοι – Όλη η Αλήθεια'). In its judgement, the court noted that Law 927/1979 must be interpreted restrictively and in light of the provisions of Article 14(1) (expression) and Article 16(1) (art, science, research and teaching) of the constitution and Article 10(1) (expression) of the ECHR, through which the freedom of expression is established as well as the freedom of art, science, research and teaching. The court placed a tight restriction on the implementation of the anti-racist law, citing free expression as justification for such restrictions given the particular significance it attached to such freedoms. However, it did note that free expression must be exercised in light of the obligations which arise from, amongst others, Article 2 of the constitution on the obligation of the state to protect human value, a provision which also incorporates the need to respect the racial and ethnic origin of a person. However, the court found Plevris not guilty, not due to the significance of free speech but, rather, that his book was directed against Zionists and not Jews who so did not constitute a racial group.[9]

3.1.2 Freedom of Assembly

Article 11 of the constitution provides that 'Greeks shall have the right to assemble peaceably and unarmed.'[10] Law 4703/2002 on Public Outdoor Assemblies defines, for the purposes of that law, a public assembly as a pre-organised event arranged for a common goal, particularly for a common demonstration, expression of opinions, making of requests of any nature or decision-making. Presidential Decree 141/1991 on the Competences of Force and Service Actions of the staff of the Ministry of Public Order and issues of Organising Services defines an assembly as a pre-arranged concentration of many people for the same reason for the purposes of decision-making and common action. Article 11(2) of the constitution holds that the police may be present only at outdoor public assemblies and that such assemblies may be prohibited 'by a reasoned police authority decision, in general if a serious threat to public security is imminent, and in a specific area, if a serious disturbance of social and economic life is threatened, as specified

---

8   Case 3/2010.
9   Case 913/2009.
10 Οι Έλληνες έχουν το δικαίωμα να συνέρχονται ήσυχα και χωρίς όπλα.

by law.'[11] Law 794/1971 on Public Assemblies provides for peaceful and unarmed assembly.[12] This statute was passed during the years of the Junta but remains in force today. It has several unconstitutional provisions which are no longer valid. Article 1(4) provides that this law is applicable only to pre-organised assemblies whilst the prohibition of instantaneous assemblies is incumbent on the free judgement of the police. The organiser of the assembly is also considered its president and this person must inform the police of the time and place of the assembly.[13] Article 6(1) therein reiterates what is held in part (2) of Article 11 of the constitution, namely that the police may prohibit a public outdoor assembly if it is determined that there is an issue of endangering public order and security, insofar as its prevention cannot be achieved through softer police measures. Softer measures may include those provided in part (4) of the article and include a change of time or place of the assembly. Any restrictions to an assembly must be communicated to the president of the assembly at least eight hours before the assembly is to take place.[14] Further requirements that need to be met in order to hold an assembly are included in this article, such as certain prohibited areas where no assembly may take place, the maximum amount of persons that can participate in an assembly and the fact that assemblies may only be made up of persons on foot. Article 9 of this law provides for punishment in the form of imprisonment and a monetary fine if, amongst other things, the organisers and/or members of the assembly do not inform the police of the assembly or carry out an assembly which has been deemed prohibited or if they continue to carry out the assembly which the police has dismantled. Presidential Decree 73/2020 on the Regulation of Public Outdoor Assemblies also provides for peaceful assemblies. Further, Article 171 of the Criminal Code provides that whoever takes part in a prohibited public assembly is punished with imprisonment of up to six months or a monetary fine. Further, if the competent military or civil authority calls for the assembly to be dismantled and a participant of such an assembly does not follow such instructions after the third request, he or she is punished with imprisonment or a monetary fine. Article 189 of the Criminal Code provides for the punishment of persons participating in violent assembly/carrying out and/or inciting violent activities. In addition

---

11 Μόνο στις δημόσιες υπαίθριες συναθροίσεις μπορεί να παρίσταται η αστυνομία. Οι υπαίθριες συναθροίσεις μπορούν να απαγορευτούν με αιτιολογημένη απόφαση της αστυνομικής αρχής, γενικά, αν εξαιτίας τους επίκειται σοβαρός κίνδυνος για τη δημόσια ασφάλεια, σε ορισμένη δε περιοχή, αν απειλείται σοβαρή διατάραξη της κοινωνικοοικονομικής ζωής, όπως νόμος ορίζει.

12 Article 1(1) and Article 11 of Law 749/1971.

13 Article 3(4) Law 794/1971.

14 Article 5(5) Law 794/1971.

to the above, Presidential Decree 73/2020 on the Regulation of Public Outdoor Assemblies deals with the competences of the police in relation to dealing with assemblies, providing for issues such as the use of force and the distinction of public and private assemblies.

In light of the above, Greece permits peaceful assemblies, limits the powers of the state to interfere in private assemblies and outlines the temporal and contextual frameworks in which the police may interfere with violent assemblies. However, in the 2015 Concluding Observations of the ICERD to Greece, the Committee noted its concern regarding human rights violations committed by the police towards demonstrators and the lack of investigations into perpetrators. In addition, it noted that during demonstrations, groups of persons such as journalists and peaceful demonstrators were 'threatened, intimidated and harassed by members of extremist groups such as Golden Dawn.'[15]

3.1.3 Non-Discrimination

The Greek constitution contains a general non-discrimination clause in Article 5(2). This holds that 'all persons living within the Greek territory shall enjoy full protection of their life, honour and liberty irrespective of nationality, race or language and of religious or political beliefs. Exceptions shall be permitted only in cases provided by international law.'[16] However, before the transposition of EU Equal Treatment Directives 2000/78/EC and 2000/43/EC into the national legal system through Law 3304/2005, the anti-discrimination framework of this country was abstract, with the general non-discrimination provision of the constitution being the only source of law on the issue. As such, Law 3304/2005 'fills a conspicuous lacuna in the Greek Legal System.'[17] Following the passing of the 2005 law, the abstract depiction of the principle was put into effect, always in the areas and *vis-à-vis* the target groups set out by Directives 2000/43/EC and 2000/78/EC.

---

15 Human Rights Committee Concluding Observations – Greece, CCPR/C/GRC/CO/2 (3 December 2015) 8.

16 Όλοι όσοι βρίσκονται στην Ελληνική Επικράτεια απολαμβάνουν την απόλυτη προστασία της ζωής, της τιμής και της ελευθερίας τους, χωρίς διάκριση εθνικότητας, φυλής, γλώσσας και θρησκευτικών ή πολιτικών πεποιθήσεων. Εξαιρέσεις επιτρέπονται στις περιπτώσεις που προβλέπει το διεθνές δίκαιο.

17 European Network of Legal Experts in the Non-discrimination Field, Athanasios Theodoridis, 'Report on Measures to Combat Discrimination – Directives 2000/43/EC and 2000/78/EC – Country Report 2013 – State of affairs up to 1st January 2014' 8.

Article 1 of the Greek non-discrimination law holds that its purpose is the establishment of a general anti-discrimination framework in relation to racial or ethnic origin as well as an anti-discrimination framework in relation to other grounds such as religion, disability, age or status in relation to employment. Article 4 prohibits discrimination in relation to the 'access to and supply of goods and services which are available to the public, including housing' but only in respect of race and ethnic origin, a minimum standard set out by the racial equality directive. Further, Article 16(1) provides for criminal sanctions in the event of discrimination in the realm of accessing goods and services. This provision holds that

> whoever violates the prohibition of discriminatory treatment on the grounds of ethnic or racial origin or religious or other beliefs, disability, age or sexual orientation, with respect to the supply of goods or the offer of services to the public is punished with six months' imprisonment and a fine of 1000 – 1500 Euros.

Article 4(2) holds that the law is applicable to differences based on nationality or to the regulation of the entrance and of third country nationals or stateless persons or the treatment linked to their legal status as third country nationals or stateless persons. This is reiterated in Article 8(2). This law is applicable to the public and private spheres.[18] The law mandates three institutions for the promotion of the principle of equal treatment, one of which is the Ombudsperson, who is entrusted with the promotion of equal treatment regardless of racial or ethnic origin, religious or other beliefs, age, disability or sexual orientation in the public sector.

Thus, taking into account the provisions of Article 4(1) and 16(1) in relation to non-discrimination in relation to accessing goods and services, insofar as this discrimination is based on racial or ethnic origin, two issues pertaining to Golden Dawn may arise. Firstly, that there exists a national non-discrimination framework which may be used to punish the discriminatory activities of Golden Dawn, such as the soup kitchen and blood donations for Greeks only. Secondly, that, notwithstanding the countless number of such activities that have taken place even after the enforcement of the non-discrimination law, this law has never been used for the collective activities of Golden Dawn. Instead, prosecution of such discrimination has occurred in two cases, only one of which could

---

18   Article 4(1) Law 3304/2005.

rely on the non-discrimination law, for reasons discussed below. Firstly, in 2013, a bus driver of a transport company of the city of Thessaloniki forced two passengers of African descent to get off the bus for no apparent reason. When the other passengers criticised this behaviour, the driver provocatively declared that he was a Golden Dawn supporter. An association, the Nazi-Free Thessaloniki Assembly, filed a complaint to the Organisation of Public Transportation of Thessaloniki. The case resulted in the intervention of the Misdemeanours Prosecutor of Thessaloniki who ordered a preliminary inquiry into the case. The court found the perpetrator guilty of denying access to services on racial grounds, holding that the bus driver's conduct offended the victims' dignity and created an intimidating, humiliating or offensive environment, without however referring to the term 'harassment.'[19] It ordered his ten-month imprisonment suspended for three years and a fine of 1,000 Euros.[20] This was the first time that Article 16, which provides for criminal penalties for discriminatory behaviour in the supply of goods and services, was enforced, reflecting a nine-year delay from the law's inception.[21] Secondly, in 2014, a Greek doctor and member of Golden Dawn posted a 'Jews not Welcome' sign outside his office and was subsequently arrested for inciting racial discrimination, in violation of anti-racist Law 972/1979.[22] This incident falls within the framework of Law 3004/2005 as the doctor, through his sign, ousted an entire ethnic and/or religious group from the provision of his services. However, the Prosecutor would have to pursue this case in the realm of Law 972/1979 which can be instigated *ex officio*, due to the fact that there was no identified victim of the aforementioned conduct. Therefore, since a case cannot be brought before judicial bodies without a designated victim under the anti-discrimination law, the only path available in the realm of ethnic and racial discrimination is the anti-racist law. Thus, whilst there exists another option in the framework of supply of goods and services for persons discriminated against due to their race or ethnicity, even if no consenting victim is identified for purposes

19 Hellenic League for Human Rights Press Release On the Conviction of the Bus Driver: <http://www.hlhr.gr/?MDL=pages&SiteID=1027> [Accessed 23 February 2021].
20 Ibid.
21 To Vima: 'A Bus Driver Removed Two Migrants from the Bus' (12 April 2012) <http://www.tovima.gr/society/article/?aid=507428> [Accessed 23 February 2021].
22 European network of Legal Experts in the Non-Discrimination Field: Prosecution of Golden Dawn Doctor (summary): <http://www.equalitylaw.eu/index.php?option=com _edocma n&task=document.viewdoc&id=1406&Itemid=295> [Accessed 23 February 2021].

of a trial, no such alternative is available for the other groups protected by equal treatment legislation. So, the necessity of a consenting victim is a direct result of the provisions of the directives and not a deviation by the state from its European obligations. Either way, such characteristics of the law are considered by institutions, such as ECRI, to constitute shortcomings that directly affect the practical applicability and scope of the equal treatment framework of member states which choose to apply the directives' provisions as minimally as possible.

Chapter 4

The Far-Right Movement and Criminal Law

4.1 Law 927/1979 – Anti-Racist Legislation

Law 927/1979 is the central piece of legislation which seeks to combat racism as manifested through speech and activities. The Greek legal system has had a piece of legislation tackling hateful speech and activities directed at racial and ethnic groups since 1979 and religious groups since 1984. This law was amended in 2014, with some of the amendments restricting the offences and creating higher thresholds.

Although the law is on racial discrimination, following the 2014 amendments, it incorporated grounds such as disability as a protected characteristic and, therefore, deals with a broader range of issues, falling outside the framework of racial discrimination. The report on the law's evaluation stated that the law was rarely implemented and deemed insufficient due to the serious challenges faced by the country in the particular temporal framework in which the amendments were being discussed. The report refers to issues such as the transition into a multicultural society and the equal protection of all persons regardless of characteristics such as physical or cultural ones. For these reasons, it was considered necessary to adopt a new and improved piece of legislation to tackle, in a more effective manner, manifestations of racist and xenophobic behaviour.[1] The explanatory report refers to the risk of violating the freedom of expression when seeking to criminalise racist and xenophobic manifestations and referred to provisions that should be followed including, *inter alia*, Articles 10, 14 and 17 of the ECHR.[2] The passing of the law

---

1   Explanatory Report for the Proposed Law on Combating Racism and Xenophobia, para. 4.
2   Ibid. para. 6.

DOI: 10.4324/9781003289302-4

came with 'intense political controversy'[3] with several political parties putting forth different draft laws before agreeing upon the final version. The law has been condemned before and after its passing, mainly due to concerns over free expression. For example, Greek academics, in a written statement signed by 139 academics, expressed their reservation to Article 2 at the stage of its deliberation.[4] In fact, during the deliberations on the bill, one of the arguments against its passing was that its provisions violate free speech, as reflected in the public deliberation on the law.[5] The way in which the state tackles the issue of free expression within the realm of the law under consideration becomes clear in its report following the public deliberation at the time when the amending law was a bill. It was noted that the protection of free expression is of utmost importance and gave an example of the type of behaviour punishable under the new law, namely the incitement to violence of a mob armed with bats and chains looking for victims who do not conform with their racial, religious or cultural standards. However, this reflects the intention of the state to attach high thresholds to what is considered prohibited conduct under the law, underlining violence as a potential requirement. This goes against the position adopted, for example, by the ECtHR which, the author argues, adopts a much lower threshold of protection of freedom of expression than it should. The impact of history and censorship that existed before the metapolitefsi period has also impacted the manner in which this freedom has been viewed and developed.[6]

Law 927/1979 includes provisions on the criminalisation of, *inter alia*, hate speech, including the denial of international war crimes such as genocide. Article 1 deals with the public incitement to violence, hatred or discrimination against a person or group of persons due to their race, colour, religion, status, ethnic origin, sexual orientation, gender identity or disability if this poses a danger to public order or constitutes a threat

---

3   FRA, 'Racism, Discrimination, Intolerance and Extremism: Learning from Experiences in Greece and Hungary' (2013) 12.

4   See for example statement made by academics: Greek Reporter: 'Greek Academics against Anti-Racism Bill' (3 September 2014) <http://greece.greekreporter.com/2014/09/03/greek-academics-against-anti-racism-bill/#sthash.Ko5rxv0l.dpuf> [Accessed 1 February 2021].

5   Public Deliberation on amendment to Law 927/1979:<http://www.opengov.gr/ministryofjustice/?p=1012> [Accessed 21 February 2021].

6   Jacob Mchangama & Natalie Alkiviadou, 'Hate Speech and the European Court of Human Rights: Whatever Happened to the Right to Offend, Shock or Disturb?' (2021) Human Rights Law Review.

to the life, liberty or physical integrity of a person or persons. Article 1 does not refer to the grounds of language and citizenship. This is not a requirement of the Framework Decision but had been recommended by ECRI.[7] A person guilty of such an offence is punished with a prison sentence ranging from three months to three years and with a monetary fine of five thousand to twenty thousand Euros. Part (2) of this article deals with damage to the property of persons on grounds of their protected characteristics insofar as this may cause harm to public order. A person found guilty under Article 1(2) receives the same punishment as that provided for in Article 1(1). If the incitement results in a criminal act, the punishment increases to imprisonment of at least six months and a monetary fine of fifteen thousand to thirty thousand Euros.[8] This is below what is provided for in the Framework Decision which holds, in Article 3(2), that the aforementioned conduct should be punishable by criminal penalties of a maximum of between one and three years' imprisonment. In sum, the above provisions punish hate speech insofar as it incites, *inter alia*, violence against a person or damage to property. However, there is no definition in the national law of what is to constitute hatred, nor any jurisprudential insight into this. As well as the above, Article 1(f) criminalises hateful organisations. More particularly, this provision holds that whoever creates or participates in an organisation or league of persons in any form, which pursues the systematic perpetuation of criminal activities as described in parts (1) and (2) of the same article (harm against persons and harm against property insofar as, *inter alia*, public order is disrupted) is punished with imprisonment of three months to three years and with a monetary fine of between five thousand and twenty thousand Euros, insofar that this is not punished more severely through another provision. Although the article on prohibited organisations incorporates the possibility of a higher punishment if one is available, the fact remains that the law gives the same punishment for an individual act which may incite hate as it does for an organised movement of persons who seek to incite hate, with the element of a group denoting an organised movement, systematic activities and, potentially, more serious consequences. Nevertheless, Article 1(4) on prohibited organisations is a significant tool to combat organised and semi-organised far-right movements. Article 1(2) of the old law prohibited the establishment and participation in organisations

---

7   European Commission against Racism and Intolerance: Report on Greece (24 February 2015) para. 12.
8   Article 1(3) Law 927/1979.

which promote propaganda or actions pertaining to racial discrimination. With the 2014 amendments, the relevant provision extends the range of target groups which are to be protected from prohibited organisations, and clarifies that an organisation can take any form. The new provision holds that prohibited organisations are ones which systematically carry out the activities of parts (1) and (2) of the article, with all the restrictions and qualifications that come with them. However, it should be reiterated that, given the sanctity provided to political parties under the Greek constitution, it can reasonably be assumed that the prohibition of organisations under the above article would not and will not extend to political parties.

Article 2 of the law deals with publicly condoning, trivialising or maliciously denying the existence or severity of international crimes such as genocide. The construction of this article became the issue of the 2016 court case against German historian Heinz Richter regarding his book in which, in relation to the Battle of Crete (with the Nazis), he argued, amongst others, that 'ruthless and barbaric practices were not only used by the invading troops but also by the Cretans who rebelled against them.' The court held that the new Article 2's provision that the crimes must have been recognised by the Greek parliament, amongst other institutions was unconstitutional. More particularly, it found that, by incorporating the provision that such crimes must have been recognised by the Greek parliament (and not the Greek judiciary), the legislature had taken the role of the judiciary by ascertaining the legal existence of crimes. Moreover, the court noted that the provision was purposely left out of the Framework Decision referring to the recognition of such crimes by decisions of international and/or national courts only. As such, the legislators exceeded the constitutional limits of the legislature, violated the constitutional principle of the legality of crimes and attempted to intervene unacceptably in judicial powers. The court also noted that laws which recognise or establish historical facts, even if they express the opinion of the majority, cannot (in a democratic and pluralist society) constitute the foundation of binding regulations which equate to legal prohibitions.[9] Either way, the punishment for crimes that fall within this article is the same as for Article 1(1). Furthermore, Article 3 deals with jurisdiction when the forum used for communication is the internet and Article 4 provides for the responsibility of legal persons or a league of persons, two points which are new additions to the law following the

---

9　Statement made by the Court regarding Heinz Richter's Case.

2014 amendments. Article 4 allows for the *ex officio* prosecution of crimes provided for in this law.[10] This is not a new provision as prosecution for racist crimes (not general hate crimes on the grounds provided for in the amended law) could be prosecuted *ex officio* since 2005.[11] However, as noted by the Ombudsperson, the power of *ex officio* prosecution has not been exercised by the authorities.[12] What is conspicuously missing from this law is the provision on aiding and abetting the crimes described in Articles 1 and 2, as required by the Framework Decision. Instead, there are some general provisions in the Criminal Code that could be relied on for such purposes. In light of the above, the 2014 amendments have impacted the country's current anti-racist legal framework of the country.

Since its inception in 1979, the anti-racist law has seldom been relied upon to combat the offences found therein,[13] with biased conduct rarely being acknowledged as such by the police and/or the courts. In fact, in 2012, the Minister of Justice recognised that 'few prosecutions for crimes regulated by Law 927/1979 have been initiated in recent years.'[14] This is particularly the case regarding the law as it stood before the 2014 amendments. However, assessing the implementation of the anti-racist law is a complex task given the lack of relevant statistics and the absence of a central hate crime database.[15] Around 60 lawsuits have been filed under the anti-racist law and almost all of these have come from the Greek Helsinki monitor but very few have resulted in a conviction. The law was relied upon in the 2010 case against Constantinos Plevris, founder of the party 4 August and Front Line, and member of LAOS and the newspaper *Eleftheros Kosmos* for his book *Jews – The Whole Truth* ('Εβραίοι

---

10   *Ex officio* prosecution existed since 2001 and Article 39(4) of Law 2910/2001 on 'The Entry and Stay of Aliens in Greece. Acquisition of Greek Citizenship through Naturalisation and other Provisions.'

11   Law 3386/2005 on 'The Entry, Stay and Social Integration of Third Country Nationals in Greece' Article 71(4).

12   Ombudsperson: Special Report: 'The Phenomenon of Racist Violence in Greece and How it Can be Tackled' (Το Φαινόμενο της Ρατσιστικής Βίας στην Ελλάδα και η Αντιμετώπισή του') (September 2013).

13   CERD Concluding Observations: Greece (14 September 2009) CERD/C/GRC/CO/16-19, 31, Fundamental Rights Agency, 'Racism, Discrimination, Intolerance and Extremism: Learning from Experiences in Greece and Hungary' (2013) 11.

14   Council of Europe Commissioner for Human Rights – Report on Greece, CommDH(2013) 6, 7.

15   European Commission against Racism and Intolerance: Report on Greece (24 February 2015) para. 34.

– Όλη η Αλήθεια'). Notwithstanding that Plevris had been prosecuted *ex officio* and was convicted at first instance on the basis of Law 927/1979, receiving a 14-month suspended prison sentence, he was subsequently acquitted by the Athens Appeal Court in 2009.[16] A motion for cassation was dismissed.[17] The Athens Appeal Court held that the writings were not directed at Jews 'solely because of their racial and ethnic origin; but mainly because of their aspirations to world power, the methods they use to achieve these aims and their conspiracy activities.'[18] This is notwithstanding the fact that the book included extracts such as:

> Adolf Hitler: The tragic leader of the German Third Reich is certainly the most impressive leadership figure of the modern age ... Human history will blame Adolf Hitler for the following: 1. He could have rid Europe of the Jews but did not; 2. He did not use the special chemical weapons, which only Germany possessed, to gain a victory ... Because of the defeat of Germany then, the White Race and Europe are at risk now ... The day will come when Europeans will either dominate or be destroyed. Either way they will acknowledge that Hitler was right.[19]

Such an extract, one of many equivalent extracts, demonstrates the weakness in the Supreme Court's argument that the book was not directed towards Jews because of their racial and ethnic origin. The Supreme Court dismissed the appeal for cassation in the interests of law, placing great importance on free speech.[20] The Council of Europe Commissioner for Human Rights noted that the judiciary did 'not manage to effectively apply Law 927/1979'[21] in this case.

---

16   Case 913/2009.

17   Case 3/2010.

18   Case 913/2009: 'Ο κατηγορούμενος δεν στρέφεται κατά των Εβραίων, μόνο λόγω της φυλετικής και εθνικής καταγωγής τους αλλά κυρίως λόγω των επιδιώξεών τους για παγκόσμια κυριαρχία, των μεθόδων που χρησιμοποιούν για την ευόδωση αυτών και τη συνωμοτική τους δράση.'

19   Konstantinos Plevris *Jews – The Whole Truth* ('Εβραίοι – Όλοι η Αλήθεια') (1st edn. Electron 2006) 881.

20   Case 3/2010.

21   Council of Europe Commissioner for Human Rights – Report on Greece, CommDH(2013) 6, 8.

In Case 65738/2014,[22] the court found a member and parliamentary candidate of Golden Dawn guilty of inciting racial violence against migrants in the area of Agios Panteleimonas in front of a camera. He said that 'we are ready to open the ovens ... To make soaps. Not for the people ... since we may fall ill ... we will take their hair and will sell it at Monastiraki.' These were some of the phrases he used to talk about migrants in the area. The court recognised that these statements were exaggerations but held that they demonstrated his conviction publicly to provoke people to cause harm to immigrants. His racist motive was recognised and he was sentenced to one year of imprisonment under the anti-racist law. Further, on 16 February 2016, the Supreme Court requested parliament to lift the immunity of three MPs of Golden Dawn so that they could be charged under the anti-racist law in relation to leaflets they disseminated which included phrases such as 'Illegal Immigrants Out' and 'Greece belongs to Greece.' Also in its newspaper and in other sources, it referred to an assembly it carried out entitled 'a protest against illegal immigrants. No to racism against Greeks.' It must be noted that these particular statements of Golden Dawn are much lower on the hierarchy of hate than its rhetoric over the years. However, no efforts were effectively made to tackle these through the anti-racist legislation. In fact, it is debatable whether the 2016 case and the statements of the party do, in fact, fall within the realm of Article 1 of the law. Either way, this case potentially demonstrates a shift in the state's approach.

Therefore, although there was a legislative framework that could have been used against acts of the far-right since 1979, this has rarely been used to tackle far-right manifestations, with the Council of Europe Commissioner of Human Rights noting 'the serious gap in training and awareness concerning anti-racism legislation and practice for police, prosecutors and judges.'[23] The investigation of bias at the stage at which a complaint is filed is of utmost importance since time and again it has been noted that bias motivation is not recorded by the police, even if they are confronted with a hate crime victim.[24] In relation to this, the Police Circular 7100/4/3 of 2006 is a useful tool for the adequate and effective investigation of such bias. The circular requires that the police

22 Case 65738/2014.
23 Council of Europe Commissioner for Human Rights – Report on Greece, CommDH(2013) 6, 9.
24 Fundamental Rights Agency, 'Racism, Discrimination, Intolerance and Extremism: Learning from Experiences in Greece and Hungary' (2013) 11.

investigate the motivation of a crime, collect relevant information and report hate crime incidents and record, amongst other things, the racial, ethnic and religious groups of the victim where relevant. However, this Circular was not accompanied by training and other methods to ensure its implementation and, as noted by the Ombudsperson, it has remained unused.[25] So, as is the case with the anti-racist legislation, significant tools available to the state to challenge the far-right have remained unused.[26] In addition to the limitations that emanate from lack of awareness and expertise lies the lack of trust in law enforcement agencies, particularly amongst victims of hate crime which is a result of the incidents of ill treatment of migrants and Roma especially by law enforcement officials and, at the same time, the lack of adequate investigations into hate crime.[27] The lack of trust in the police also emanates from the 'persistent and continuing allegations, some of which were officially investigated, of collusion between police officers and Golden Dawn.'[28] The link between the police and Golden Dawn is a serious issue that also arose during the onset of the party's trial. In addition, there have been several reports of the police requesting alleged victims of hate crimes to pay the amount of one hundred Euros for the purposes of lodging their complaint. This practice went against the law given that Article 46 of the Code of Criminal Procedure requests that such a fee is to be paid for cases which are not prosecuted *ex officio*. Article 5 of the 2014 amending law incorporated a provision which directly excluded the payment of such fees for filing a hate crime complaint. Furthermore, up until 2014, national law placed undocumented migrants who were victims of hate crime at risk of detention and deportation. As a result, such migrants were reluctant to report the crime to the police or even to visit public health

---

25 Ombudsperson: Special Report: 'The Phenomenon of Racist Violence in Greece and How it Can be Tackled' (Το Φαινόμενο της Ρατσιστικής Βίας στην Ελλάδα και η Αντιμετώπισή του') (September 2013) 44.

26 Fundamental Rights Agency, 'Racism, Discrimination, Intolerance and Extremism: Learning from Experiences in Greece and Hungary' (2013) 12.

27 Council of Europe Commissioner for Human Rights – Report on Greece, CommDH(2013) 6, 11.

28 European Commission against Racism and Intolerance: Report on Greece (24 February 2015) para. 58, European Network of Legal Experts in the Non-Discrimination Field, Athanasios Theodoridis, 'Report on Measures to Combat Discrimination – Directives 2000/43/EC and 2000/78/EC – Country Report 2013 – State of affairs up to 1st January 2014' 133.

care services.[29] However, Ministerial Decision 30651/2014 allows for the issuance of a residence permit on humanitarian grounds to migrants who are victims of or key witnesses to hate crime and are valid until the case is closed or the final court judgement is passed.[30] For a permit to be issued, criminal proceedings must have been initiated. Although this is a positive step which develops the law in a manner in which it can provide enhanced protection to victims of hate crime and subsequently challenge the far-right, as argued by ECRI, it would have been more effective for there to be an 'automatic suspension of the deportation orders rather than leaving it to ministerial discretion.'[31] Embarak Abouzid, the victim of the attempted homicide in Piraeus by members of Golden Dawn (the Egyptian fishermen case), was the first person to receive a humanitarian permit under this provision.[32]

As such, Greece has had anti-racist legislation since 1979 which renders criminally punishable rhetoric and activities which fall within the sphere of the far-right. This piece of legislation has undergone certain amendments since that time, bringing changes such as the incorporation of religion as a protected characteristic and in 2014 underwent major changes for the purposes of harmonising national law with the Council Framework Decision 2008/913/JHA. These amendments brought about several changes to the current law, broadening its scope in some respects, such as by incorporating a larger number of protected characteristics but also making it more speech protective as is manifested in the necessary interrelation between hateful speech and public disorder. In addition, Greece recognised the need to crack down on hate crime, albeit not directly recognising the correlation between such crimes and Golden Dawn. Such recognition is manifested in, for example, the 2006 Police Circular on bias motivation and in the establishment of regional departments in Athens and Thessaloniki and special units to tackle racist violence which have the duty to conduct investigations into racist crime, carry out an *ex officio* investigation and receive complaints in person or through a hotline.[33] However, there 'is little evidence so far of their

29 Human Rights First, 'We're not Nazis, but…The Rise of Hate Parties in Hungary and Greece and Why America should Care' (August 2014) 97.

30 Ministerial Decision 30651 (5 June 2014).

31 European Commission against Racism and Intolerance: Report on Greece (24 February 2015) para. 84.

32 Civil Action (Case files ABM Φ2013/3990, ABM Φ2012/979 and 979A) 15.

33 Fundamental Rights Agency, 'Racism, Discrimination, Intolerance and Extremism: Learning from Experiences in Greece and Hungary' (2013) 14.

effectiveness.'[34] Moreover, the anti-racist legislation remains essentially unused with some sporadic reliance on the law whilst other measures, such as the anti-racist units and the Police Circular on bias motivation, have not brought about a significant change or results. Moreover, there are real and practical obstacles, such as the link between the police and Golden Dawn, especially and more evidently before the latter's trial, which prevented victims from filing complaints.

4.2 Aggravating, Sentencing and Hate Crimes

Since 2008, the aggravating circumstance of a crime has been incorporated into Article 79(3) of the criminal law which provided[35] that carrying out an act of ethnic, racial, religious hatred or hatred based on the victim's status constitutes an aggravating circumstance. Since 2013,[36] the grounds of aggravation were extended to cover the colour, sexual orientation and gender identity of the victim. In addition, it stipulated that a sentence in such a situation cannot be suspended. Article 79 provided courts with the opportunity to take into consideration the aforementioned circumstances at the time of sentencing. This provision acknowledged the particular weight of such a circumstance and allowed courts to take it into account so as to hand down the maximum sentence possible without the possibility of its suspension. However, it did not provide the court with the opportunity to give a higher sentence than it could hand down for the equivalent crime which had no bias motive. The non-use of this provision can be demonstrated in some cases. A 2014 case involved a Golden Dawn member, Kontomos, who participated in the fascist attack of a hit squad against a hair salon run by a Pakistani immigrant.[37] He, along with eight others, entered the salon and attacked the two Pakistani employees and one Greek client. They then exited the salon and threw

---

34 European Commission against Racism and Intolerance: Report on Greece (24 February 2015) para. 77.

35 Article 23(1) of Law 3719/2008 'Amendments for the Family, the Child, the Society and other Provisions' provides that the commission of an offence motivated by ethnic, racial or religious hatred or hatred on account of a different sexual orientation constitutes an aggravating circumstance.

36 Article 66 of Law 4139/2013 on Addictive Substances and other Provisions.

37 There exist several other cases in which the violent actions of Golden Dawn have been prosecuted by the courts without the recognition of the racist motives have been made; see: < http://www.efsyn.gr/arthro/oi-katadikes-tis-hrysis-aygis> [Accessed 14 January 2021].

a self-made Molotov bomb into the property. It must be noted that similar attacks continued to occur over the following weeks in the same area. This case did not result in the investigation of racist motives by the police. Kontomos was sentenced to 14 years and three months of imprisonment as an accomplice in an attempted homicide, dangerous bodily harm, robbery and possession of explosives. However, as with the police, the court did not use the provision of aggravation due to a racist motive, as contained in Article 79(3) applicable at the material time.[38] Further, in 2012, the Magistrates Court only imposed a suspended sentence of eight months and a pecuniary fine of two hundred Euros on a Golden Dawn member who had violently attacked a member of the Muslim minority in Thrace.[39] However, there are some exceptions to the non-use of the legal framework but also to the habitual inaction of the authorities. In the 2014 case of Shehzad Luqman, a migrant from Pakistan, who was stabbed to death by two members of Golden Dawn when he was on his bicycle going to work, authorities found Golden Dawn material and weapons at the perpetrators' houses. The court recognised Article 79(3) and the 'racist fury' of the perpetrators and found them guilty of, amongst other offences, homicide with intent, illegal possession carrying and use of weapons. The court did not recognise any mitigating factors and handed down the highest sentences possible, more particularly life sentences for both for the intentional homicide plus 32 months for the other offences.[40] Although the court placed the sentencing of the perpetrators within the framework of a racist motive, in their words, racist fury, an interesting point to make was their reference to Golden Dawn. More particularly, the court held that their membership of this party was not relevant to criminal responsibility. This is a weak point of the judgement and reflective of the general stance of the judiciary towards Golden Dawn's actions, since they were not willing to recognise the link between the perpetration of criminal acts and Golden Dawn as a violent entity. Following Luqman's murder, Amnesty International announced that this crime was not an isolated incident and that urgent measures needed to be taken.[41] This case was subsequently included in the case-file

---

38   Case 114/2014.
39   Council of Europe Commissioner for Human Rights – Report on Greece, CommDH(2013) 6, 18.
40   Case 398/2014.
41   Amnesty International Press Release: The Recognition of Racist Motive in the case of Shehzad Luqman (Η αναγνώριση του ρατσιστικού κινήτρου στην υπόθεση Σαχζάτ Λουκμάν)

against Golden Dawn as presented to the Supreme Court.[42] In Case 1079/2014, the court found four members of Golden Dawn guilty of attacking Pakistani immigrants working at an olive factory. According to the decision they 'acted with xenophobic and racist feelings.'[43] In Case 60084/2013,[44] two members of Golden Dawn were found guilty of the arson of a bar owned by a Cameroonian national. The court found that their actions were 'prompted by hate due to the racial and ethnic origin of the civil plaintiff' and sentenced them to 41 months' imprisonment. Notwithstanding some positive steps and use of the aggravation provision, the fact remains that Article 79(3) has rarely been used.[45]

Part (3) of Article 79 was replaced by Article 10 of Law 4285/2014, which brought about further changes to the Criminal Code in relation to hate crimes. More particularly, Article 10 incorporates Article 81A, an article entitled 'racist crime' and provides that:

> If the act is carried out of hate due to the victim's race, colour, religion, descent, ethnic origin, sexual orientation, gender identity or disability, sentencing increases as follows:
>
> a)   in the event of a misdemeanour, for which the foreseen sentence is between ten days and one year' imprisonment, the lowest sentence is increased by six months and by one year in the rest of the cases of a misdemeanour.
> b)   in the event of a felony, for which the foreseen sentence is between five and ten years' imprisonment, the lowest sentence is increased by two years and by three years for the rest of the cases of a felony; and
> c)   fines are doubled
>
> The lowest sentence is not suspendable

(2013): <https://www.amnesty.gr/news/press/article/15963/i-anagnorisi-toy-ratsistikoy -kinitroy-stin-ypothesi-toy-sahzat-loykman> [Accessed 25 February 2021].

42   *Attorneys of the Civil Action: Memo of the Civil Action of the Anti-Fascist Movement for the Trial of Golden Dawn (Υπόμνημα της Πολιτικής Αγωγής του Αντιφασιστικού Κινήματος για τη Δίκη της Χρυσής Αυγής)* (1st edn. Marxist Bookshop, Athens 2015) 137.
43   Case 398/2014.
44   Case 60084/2013.
45   European Commission against Racism and Intolerance: Report on Greece (24 February 2015) para. 60.

Thus, although this article is entitled 'Racist Crimes,' it is actually a provision on hate crime. As such, this article is significant as it embeds hate crime as a provision in itself within the Greek Criminal Code and not simply within the ambit of aggravating circumstances, as previously set out. Also, this provision provides for higher sentences for hate crimes as opposed to the old law which simply enabled the courts to provide the highest sentence possible without suspension. Further, Article 10 amends Article 61 of the Criminal Code, incorporating the situation described in Article 81A above as a reason for depriving the perpetrator of his/her civil rights for one to five years. On the one hand this is a positive amendment, on the other, however, the issue of hate crime continues directly to link the issue of hatred to sentencing and does not set out, for example, the consideration of a racist backdrop of a crime to be considered throughout judicial proceedings. No amendments were made, for example, to the Code of Criminal Procedure in relation to, for example, the consideration of a racist backdrop of a crime at the investigation stage. Although the 2006 Police Circular exists on the consideration of hateful motivations, an amendment to the aforementioned codes and an adoption of the approach that the elements of a hate crime are to be considered throughout the entire procedure and not just in relation to sentencing would have ensured a more effective legal framework in relation to such crimes. As noted by ECRI, authorities must closely monitor the way in which Article 81A is used by the courts and whether it overcomes the problems caused by Article 79(3).[46]

4.3 Advances, Amendments and Alterations in the Sphere of Criminal Law

The Greek legal order has undergone several developments over the past few years such as the 2014 amendments which included, amongst other things, an enhanced recognition of hate crimes. It has also undergone other significant amendments which should, theoretically, facilitate the access to justice for victims of hate crime. For example, since 2001 crimes incorporated in the anti-racist law can be prosecuted *ex officio*, even though, as reflected in the examination of available jurisprudence, this is not relied on by authorities. Further, a Special Prosecutor was appointed

---

46 European Commission against Racism and Intolerance: Report on Greece (24 February 2015) para. 14.

for the investigation of racist crimes in the region of Athens.[47] Before the establishment of this body, legal practitioners had indicated to the Council of Europe Commissioner for Human Rights that such a development would allow for the consideration of a racist motive from the onset of proceedings, rather than merely considering such a motive at the end of the trial in terms of sentencing.[48] However, this post only exists for the region of Athens with the Council of Europe Commissioner for Human Rights recommending its extension into other areas to ensure adequate and geographical fairness in relation to the effective implementation of the anti-racist law,[49] insofar as the Special Prosecutor can bring about such results. Further, Presidential Decree 132/2012 established several departments and bureaus for combatting violence based on racial, ethnic or religious hatred. More particularly, two anti-racist departments were established, one in the region of Attica and one in Thessaloniki whilst 68 bureaus were established in different police departments throughout the country.[50] They can carry out investigations into racist attacks, carry out an *ex officio* investigation and receive complaints through a hotline.[51] Although this is a positive development on a theoretical level, in 2015, ECRI noted that there was little evidence of their effective functioning.[52] In addition, the barriers to reporting a hate crime have been partly tackled through Article 44(1) of Law 3386/2004 as amended. This article allows the Ministry of Interior to grant a residence permit on humanitarian grounds to migrants (third country nationals) who are victims of crimes provided for in Articles 1 and 2 of Law 927/1979 and Article 16(1) of Law 3304/2005[53] in the event that a criminal prosecution has

---

47 Ministry of Justice – General Secretariat of Transparency and Human Rights – Human Rights – National Action Plan (Δικαιώματα του Ανθρώπου – Εθνικό Σχέδιο Δράσης) 2014–2016 (2014).

48 Council of Europe Commissioner for Human Rights – Report on Greece, CommDH(2013) 6, 65.

49 Council of Europe Commissioner for Human Rights – Report on Greece, CommDH(2013) 6, 1.

50 Ombudsperson: Special Report: 'The Phenomenon of Racist Violence in Greece and How it Can be Tackled' (Το Φαινόμενο της Ρατσιστικής Βίας στην Ελλάδα και η Αντιμετώπισή του') (September 2013) 29.

51 European Commission against Racism and Intolerance: Report on Greece (24 February 2015) para. 77.

52 Council of Europe Commissioner for Human Rights – Report on Greece, CommDH(2013)6, 81.

53 It sets out criminal penalties for offences provided for in this law.

commenced and up until the moment that a final judgement has been delivered.[54]

As such, within the realm of anti-racist legislation, it can be said that Greece, albeit with certain limitations, has an adequate framework of criminal law that can be relied upon to tackle the activities and rhetoric of the far-right. It cannot be doubted that over the past few years this country has taken significant steps in improving this particular aspect of its legal order, incorporating the 2008 EU Framework Decision, albeit restrictively in some areas, establishing a Special Prosecutor for racist crimes and seeking to overcome certain reporting obstacles by allowing for the granting of residence permits on humanitarian grounds for victims of hate crime. In its 2009 Concluding Observations, the CERD noted that Greece was 'not effectively implementing legal provisions aimed at eliminating racial discrimination and in particular those relating to the prosecution and punishment of racially motivated crimes.'[55] The Council of Europe Commissioner for Human Rights shared this view, arguing that there is an 'ineffective application or non-application of the existing anti-racism legislation'[56] and referring to the lack of training of competent authorities as the key reason for this reality.[57] In addition to the lapses between theory and practice when it comes to Greek legislation and the non-application of the law when it comes to challenging the far-right, there is one more issue that is of a more general nature that also comes into play when considering the efficacy of the current legal framework for purposes of tackling the far-right. That is the issue of access to justice. The first element of this is the fact that Greece has slow judicial proceedings. A fact that illustrates this point is that out of the 662 judgements delivered against Greece by the ECtHR up until the end of 2012, over half, and particularly 438, concerned the excessive length of judicial proceedings.[58] The second element relates to the issue of legal aid as regulated by Law 3226/2002 on the Provision of Legal Aid to persons

---

54 Provided that the person is not a risk to public order and safety. In case such persons are under medical treatment, the residence permit is granted until the termination of the treatment.

55 CERD Concluding Observations: Greece CERD/C/GRC/CO/16-19 (14 September 2009) 2.

56 Council of Europe Commissioner for Human Rights – Report on Greece, CommDH(2013) 6, 69.

57 Ibid.

58 European Court of Human Rights See Annual Report 2011, p. 160 and Annual Report 2012, p. 152.

of low income and other provisions which include legal aid to migrants and stateless persons. For the purposes of ensuring that such victims are considered on an equal footing in the national legal system, this point should be rectified. As such, along with the particular issues above which prevent the effective legal challenging of the far-right, its actors and elements, the issue of effectively accessing justice is of utmost importance as only with an improvement in this situation will victims of the far-right be able to find justice through the prosecution of the perpetrators.

4.4 Criminal Organisation – Prohibition of Establishment, Leadership and Participation

Article 187 of the Criminal Code on criminal organisations is particularly significant for this book given that it is the provision through which the state punished Golden Dawn's leadership and members. Article 187(1) of the Criminal Code punishes with imprisonment of up to ten years whosoever establishes or becomes a member of a criminal organisation. Whoever leads such an organisation receives a prison sentence of at least ten years.[59] The article holds that a criminal organisation is an entity which includes three or more members that aims at committing an array of offences including, *inter alia*, homicide with intent, grievous bodily harm, arson and kidnapping.[60] The establishment of a criminal organisation is the provision of guidance and help with the steps necessary for the recruitment of members for the creation of the organisation.[61] In relation to the establishment of a criminal organisation which comes with a lower sentence than running such an organisation, the Prosecutor's recommendation refers to it as a 'momentary crime.'[62] Throughout the trial documents, Michaloliakos is referred to as the founder and leader of Golden Dawn. Yet in the Prosecutor's recommendation, in relation to Michaloliakos, no reference is made to the aspect of establishing a criminal organisation but rather his participation and leadership of a criminal organisation. The type, details or object of such crimes do not have to be pre-determined, all that is necessary is that pursuing the perpetration of such crimes is directly linked to the establishment or functioning of

---

59   Article 187(3) Criminal Code.
60   Article 187 Criminal Code.
61   Special Investigation Department: Athens Court of Appeal: Report to the President of the Greek Parliament regarding lifting the immunity of Golden Dawn Members of Parliament, Document Number 305 (19 February 2014) 8.
62   Ibid. 13.

such a group, even if it is not required that the perpetration of such a crime reflects the will of all those who established and participate in the organisation and is not necessarily known by all members.[63] In brief, there are three elements necessary for the existence of a criminal organisation under the Criminal Code. Firstly, a qualitative element in that the group must be structured, secondly, a quantitative element in that the group must be made up of three or more persons and thirdly, a temporal element namely the requirement for ongoing action.[64] The trial documents hold that the prohibitions arising from Article 187 occur for the purposes of protecting public order and personal freedoms.[65] Moreover, the organisation must have an objective, common to the members/leaders. This can be financial, ideological or anything else.[66] Further, the Prosecutor's recommendation noted that criminal organisations are extremely dangerous due to their particular dynamic and their internal objective of committing particularly serious crimes.[67]

A significant issue is the determination of who is to be considered a member of a criminal organisation since a conceptualisation of this is important to understand the criminal responsibility of Golden Dawn members. This point is elucidated in documents from the party's trial, namely the pre-trial report and the Prosecutor's recommendation. They hold that a member of the organisation is anyone who subordinates his or her will to the will of the organisation, without his or her personal involvement in the operations of the organisation being necessary. His or her participation in the organisation is manifested by the participation in military training activities, festivities and talks, the commission of punishable acts, the propaganda of the organisation, funding of its activities, attracting new members to the organisation or any other forms of support. It is of no relevance if the decisions are taken by the majority of members or, due to the embedded principle of obedience, if they are taken by the leader, as long as any decision is considered the decision of the organisation. Mere support of the organisation's objectives extraneously does not make him or her a member. In a criminal organisation, the desire of the group for the implementation of its objectives binds all members, regardless of their involvement in the design of the criminal

---

63   Ibid. 19.
64   Ibid. 7.
65   Ibid. 11, 26, 8.
66   Ibid. 11.
67   Ibid.

acts, as long as each member is aware that he or she is contributing to the implementation of the organisation's objectives through the duties granted to him/her.[68] For the above to be applicable, the element of malice is required with the members/leaders of the groups wanting to be part of the membership/management of the group. Malice is demonstrated in the participation in all types of activities, having knowledge of crimes, accepting these crimes as desirable objectives, not repudiating such acts and remaining in the group.[69] As such, the definition of 'member' in the realm of a criminal organisation seems to denote that criminal responsibility extends to the active members of the party even if those members do not take part in the commission of a particular crime, but, as is reasonable, does not extend to those who merely support the objectives of the party (and may even vote for this party).

The Criminal Organisation provision was used to imprison members of the Revolutionary Organisation 17 November in 2003. This organisation was a violent far-left organisation which carried out its crimes for 27 years as an untraceable ghost organisation, carrying out over 90 attacks against Greek, American and European targets such as government officials. The important difference was that during the trial of 17 November, which ended on 17 December 2003,[70] the provision on terrorist organisations was not part of the Criminal Code since Article 187B became part of the Greek Criminal Code in 2005 following amendments brought about by Law 3251/2004[71] adopted in July 2004. Unlike Golden Dawn, this organisation was habitually referred to as a terrorist organisation by competent authorities,[72] the media[73] and the public, something which is not the case with Golden Dawn. One will never know whether the anti-terror provision of the Criminal Code would have been used for 17 November had it existed at the time of its trial.

---

68   Ibid. 9.
69   Ibid. 10.
70   Appeals for sentences took place in 2005–2007.
71   Law on European arrest warrants and amendment of Law 298/2001 on criminal organisations and other provisions.
72   See, for example, Police Press Release regarding 17 November (22 May 2003): <http://www.astinomia.gr/index.php?option=ozo_content&perform=view&id=1317&Itemid=171&lang= > [Accessed 20 February 2021].
73   See online articles such as: < http://www.newsbeast.gr/society/arthro/386344/ti-kanoun-simera-oi-protagonistes-tis-17-noemvri> and < http://www.newsbomb.gr/tags/tag/31957/17-noemvrh> [Accessed 20 February 2021].

4.5 Terrorist Organisations: Core Difference

Article 187B of the Criminal Code holds that

> a terrorist act is the commission of a criminal activity including, *inter alia*, homicide with intent, grievous bodily harm, arson or kidnapping in a manner or to an extent or under circumstances which may seriously harm a country or an international organisation and has the aim seriously to intimidate a population or illegally force a public authority or international organisation to carry out any act or omit to do so or to seriously harm or ruin the fundamental constitutional, political or financial infrastructure of a country or of an international organisation.

No definition in any legislative, jurisprudential or policy document exists regarding issues of threshold in relation to the above definition, such as what the severity of harm may be and what could constitute an intimidating circumstance for a population. This could potentially retract from the clarity of the definition and does not facilitate its suitable use. In brief, the difference between a criminal organisation and a terrorist organisation is that the latter seeks to carry out the criminal acts noted in the relevant section with the aim of achieving results such as population intimidation or serious harm to a country's infrastructure. On the other hand, a criminal organisation is lower on the hierarchy of harm given that it is simply termed as such as it entails three or more persons who conduct criminal activities with no overarching objective to cause collective harm as is the case with a terrorist organisation. This is notwithstanding the fact that the trial documents recognised the damage caused by Golden Dawn to, amongst others, the rule of law and the rights of others.

It could be argued, that by relying on Article 187 of the Criminal Code rather than Article 187B, the authorities did not consider the activities of Golden Dawn to meet the threshold of seriously intimidating a population and/or seriously harming or ruining the fundamental constitutional or political infrastructure[74] of Greece regardless of its reign of terror on the streets of Greece (predominantly Athens) and even though the trial documents recognise that the group's activities were destructive to, amongst other things, the rule of law.

---

74 The financial infrastructure requirement is not deemed directly applicable to Golden Dawn's actions.

Chapter 5

The International and European Frameworks

Greece signed the ICERD in 1966 and ratified it in 1970 through Legislative Decree 494/1970 on the Ratification of the Convention on the Elimination of all Forms of Racial Discrimination. It was anti-racist Law 927/1979 (subsequently amended in 2014) which sought to give effect to the ICERD. This country carried out the ratification, making no reservation to the articles therein. Article 4 of the Convention provides, *inter alia*, that State Parties 'shall declare illegal and prohibit organisations, and also organised and all other propaganda activities, which promote and incite racial discrimination, and shall recognise participation in such organisations or activities as an offence punishable by law.' This article is in direct contravention with the Greek constitutional system, which does not allow for the prohibition of political parties. It is thus surprising that the country made no reservation thereto. Further, Greece made no declaration under Article 14 of the ICERD and, as such, victims of a violation cannot seek recourse to the competent Committee through the individual complaints procedure. This directly restricts the efficacy of the document in the realm of challenging the far-right as victims cannot find recourse at the UN. This would have been particularly important for Greece given that a decision made by the CERD could have been useful in pushing the state to mobilise itself against Golden Dawn earlier. However, it is acknowledged that other reports/recommendations that have been issued by institutions such as ECRI were not taken into account. The role of Article 29 of the constitution is also reiterated here. Further, a few points will be made in relation to the conformity of the above-discussed Law 927/1979 with the ICERD and particularly Article 4 of the ICERD which prohibits, amongst other things, racist ideas, organisations and violence and is thus the most relevant to tackling the far-right as manifested in organised or semi-organised movements. Article 1(4) of Law 927/1979 as amended by Law 4285/2014 holds that the establishment or participation in an organisation or league

DOI: 10.4324/9781003289302-5

of persons of any form, which systematically seeks the perpetration of acts such as the incitement to, *inter alia*, discrimination which pose a danger to public order or constitute a threat to the life, liberty or physical integrity of the persons concerned, are to be prohibited. The reason for this discrepancy is that the same instrument, namely the anti-racist Law 927/1979, has been used to give effect both to the ICERD and the Framework Decision 2008/913/JHA. In relation to the prohibition of racist organisations, the former imposes no obligation as to, for example, the existence of an interlink between the organisation's actions and public disorder whilst the latter does not tackle the prohibition of organisations *per se*, although it does refer to the responsibility of legal as well as natural entities. Thus, the national anti-racist law takes the necessity to prohibit hateful organisations, as this emanates from the ICERD, and intertwines the optional link established by the Framework Decision insofar as particular conduct may result in, for example, public disorder. It must be noted that, before the 2014 amendments to the anti-racist law, Article 1(2) of Law 927/1979 prohibited the leading or participating in an organisation which pursues organised propaganda or activities of any kind pertaining to racial discrimination. As such, pre-2014 there were no restrictions of thresholds, making no requests for public disorder, for example, but, at the same time, offering a wider range of grounds upon which the law could be used. However, once again, the sanctity of political parties in Greek constitutional law is reiterated, restricting the use of the anti-racist law against political parties as entities.

Further, Greece ratified the ICCPR in 1997 with Law 2462/1997 on the Ratification of the ICCPR and the Optional Protocol and the Second Optional Protocol with no reservations. Although individual complaints can be communicated to the treaty body of this Convention, given that Greece ratified the Optional Protocol in 1997, recognising the competence of the Human Rights Committee to receive individual complaints, there is no jurisprudence relevant to manifestations of the far-right. The most relevant articles of the ICCPR include Article 19 on the right to freedom of expression, Article 21 on assembly, Article 22 on association (and the limitation grounds) as well as Article 20(2) which prohibits 'any advocacy of national, racial or religious hatred that constitutes incitement to discrimination, hostility or violence.'

Greece became a member of the Council of Europe in 1949. It signed the ECHR in 1950 and ratified it in November 1974 (after the dictatorship). In 1969 and during the Junta, Greece departed from the Council of Europe. After its fall, Greece became a member of the Council of Europe again and the Convention became part of national law for a second time. Protocol 12 of the Convention on the general prohibition of discrimination was signed by Greece on 4 November 2000 but has not yet been ratified. Further, on a Council of Europe level, in 2003, Greece signed the Additional Protocol concerning the Criminalisation of Acts of a Racist and Xenophobic Nature committed through Computer Systems, although it has not yet ratified this document. In the National Action Plan on Human Rights for the period 2014–2016, it was stated that the ratification of this Additional Protocol is a central objective for the purposes of improving the current legislative framework.[1] No mention is made in the Action Plan of the ratification of Protocol 12 of the ECHR.

In light of the above, the major UN instruments namely the ICERD and the ICCPR, which directly prohibit certain types of hateful rhetoric and activity and the ECHR, which limits freedoms such as that of expression, assembly and association are all part of national law. Such ratifications, in theory, have allowed for the infiltration of militant democracy into the national legal system of this country. On a practical level, militancy can be discerned in the treatment of individual and non-party rhetoric and activity but does not extend to the sphere of political parties given Article 29 of the constitution. Moreover, the relevant provisions were part of the legal system before the onset of the systematic criminality and dissemination of hateful rhetoric carried out and conducted by Golden Dawn. As such, it cannot be alleged that the country lacked in terms of legislation when it came to imposing criminal or other restrictive measures to the rhetoric and activities of Golden Dawn members. During this time, the country had the legislative capacity to prohibit Golden Dawn from further conducting its activities if it sought to interpret 'organisations' as contained in the ICERD and in the national legislation ratifying it (without reservation), in a manner which also encompasses political organisations and namely political parties, especially those using the guise of a political party to perpetrate crime and violence and spread fear amongst the community. However, the constitutional protection of political parties in Greek law renders the use of provisions such as Article 4 of the ICERD against such entities a legal impossibility. In a 2013 report, the Council of Europe Commissioner for Human Rights argued that public discussion on Golden Dawn appeared to 'ignore or not to

---

1   Ministry of Justice – General Secretariat of Transparency and Human Rights: 'Human Rights National Action Plan 2014–2016' (Δικαιώματα του Ανθρώπου – Εθνικό Σχέδιο Δράσης 2014–2016) (2014).

take duly into account a number of relevant international and European human rights standards which legally bind Greece'[2] and could have been used against Golden Dawn. The above documents and articles were not taken into account or implemented by competent authorities, up until the point where this organisation became empowered through impunity and facilitated through socio-economic circumstances, discussed above, to become a criminal organisation. The fact remains that for years Golden Dawn was acting and speaking relentlessly in direct contravention to the letter and spirit of the international and European documents referred to above. However, the fact that Golden Dawn had the status of a political party rendered its handling by the state a complex matter given the scope of the constitutional protection offered by Article 29. It would thus be simplistic merely to say that Greece turned a blind eye to its obligations as these arise from the documents. Instead, the constitutional conundrum resulting from the duality of Golden Dawn as a political party and a criminal organisation is a factor that must be taken into account. What can be argued is that despite constitutional limitations inherent in party prohibitions, the state could have acted more quickly within the sphere of individual responsibility resulting from the Criminal Code as it finally did after Fyssas's murder in 2013.

2   Council of Europe Commissioner for Human Rights – Report on Greece, CommDH (2013) 6, 6.

Chapter 6

Conclusion

The elements of the Greek legal order relevant to challenging the far-right include the anti-racist law, the Criminal Code and the anti-discrimination law. Although the far-right or comparable movements and groups are not predominantly viewed through public order legislation as they are in, for example, England and Wales, the issue of public order and the importance attached thereto, when considering tackling the far-right, is evident in the anti-racist law and the trial documents referred to above. Notwithstanding the above, the fact remains that the legislative tools available to the state to tackle the rhetoric and activities of Golden Dawn remained unused and, instead, this group carried out crimes with a high level of impunity. Even in cases pertaining to Golden Dawn violence that were brought to justice, the judiciary often steered away from looking at racist motives. The state's institutions, although aware of Golden Dawn's systemic and systematic violence, never took any serious steps to examine the relationship between Golden Dawn and the array of violent activities occurring in Greece although, in many cases, coming face to face and even acknowledging affiliation of perpetrators to Golden Dawn. This state of affairs continued up until 2013 and up until the point that the state's inactivity and non-use of the legal tools had allowed Golden Dawn to develop extensively. Here, it must also be underlined that despite the absolutist approach adopted by the Greek legal order towards political parties, this does not stand in the way of prosecuting the leadership and members of a criminal organisation, just because this entity is registered as a political party.[1] The unfortunate matter is that the Greek state waited too late to commence a process under the Criminal Code. One could argue that even the use of criminal law,

---

1 Lambros Margaritis & Konstantinos Hadjioannou 'Criminal Organisations and Political Parties' ('Εγκληματικές Οργανώσεις και Πολιτικά Κόμματα') 2 *Criminal Justice* (2014) 178.

DOI: 10.4324/9781003289302-6

rather than a direct party ban, made the state fearful of appearing to censor or limit a political party. However, this argument quickly crumbles when considering the basic tenets of a functioning democracy based on equality, non-discrimination and human rights. It could also be argued that the state strategically waited to 'build' a solid criminal case against the leaders and members of Golden Dawn. This also deteriorates quickly in light of the plethora of criminal acts of the group, known by the state, as demonstrated above.

In addition to the non-reliance on legislative tools and the institutional racism marking parts of state organs, the absolutist stance adopted by the state towards political parties has facilitated Golden Dawn's untouchability. This emanates from the reality that, in Greece, political parties, even ones with dangerous and undemocratic intentions, can register and function without any serious limitations with the only point of state intervention being when such entities cross into the threshold of a criminal organisation. Evidently the registration and (non) regulation of political parties constituted a key weakness in tackling Golden Dawn. Despite the fact that Article 29 of the constitution provides that political parties must serve a free functioning democracy and although parties need to submit a declaration of allegiance to this principle, no process is in place to check/review whether this is actually the case. This is the minor tweak this book promulgates as a middle ground for avoiding repetitions of a dangerous party in parliament (and in the case of Golden Dawn, on the streets as well). It is comparable to that proposed by the Council of Europe's Commissioner for Human Rights. This would bode sufficiently well with the procedural democratic model adopted by Greece and limit the level of constitutional militance proposed by Lowenstein. It seems to be the case that the state had omitted to pay any consideration to the qualification of Article 29(1) insofar as political parties must serve a free functioning democracy as well as its international obligations when it comes to prohibiting racist parties.

As such, Golden Dawn did not get as far as it did because of the lack of legislative and judicial tools that could be used against it and its members. Instead, the violence committed by *Golden Dawn* and the non-intervention on the part of the state (up until the murder of Fyssas) has been an anathema to (the birthplace of) democracy and to the rule of law.

Index

For Product Safety Concerns and Information please contact our EU
representative GPSR@taylorandfrancis.com
Taylor & Francis Verlag GmbH, Kaufingerstraße 24, 80331 München, Germany

9 7 8 1 0 3 2 2 6 6 6 1 9